COMMUNITY ORGANIZATION IN SOCIAL WORK

COMMUNITY ORGANIZATION IN SOCIAL WORK

By
Mrs. Sheeba Joseph
*Head
Dept. of Social Work
Bhopal School of Social Sciences
Bhopal (M.P.)
(India)*
&
Bishnu Mohan Dash
*Assistant Professor
Dept. of Social Work
Dr. Bhim Rao Ambedkar College
(University of Delhi)
Delhi (India)*

DISCOVERY PUBLISHING HOUSE PVT. LTD.
NEW DELHI-110 002

Published by:
Tilak Wasan

DISCOVERY PUBLISHING HOUSE PVT. LTD.
4383/4B, Ansari Road, Darya Ganj
New Delhi-110 002 (India)
Phone : +91-11-23279245, 43596064-65
Fax   : +91-11-23253475
E-mail : parul.wasan@gmail.com
         discoverypublishinghouse@gmail.com
web   : www.discoverypublishinggroup.com

First Edition: 2013

ISBN: 978-93-5056-372-4

Community Organization in Social Work

© 2013, **Authors**

All rights reserved. No part of this publication should be reproduced, stored in a retrieval system, or transmitted in any form or by any means: electronic, mechanical, photocopying, recording or otherwise, without the prior written permission of the authors and the publisher.

> This book has been published in good faith that the material provided by authors is original. Every effort is made to ensure accuracy of material, but the publisher and printer will not be held responsible for any inadvertent error(s). In case of any dispute, all legal matters are to be settled under Delhi jurisdiction only.

Printed at:
Dynamic Printers
Delhi

Preface

The interest to write a text-book on Community organization came to our mind when we realized that, there is a need for a simple text-book on community organization. Community organization is an important component not only at the bachelor's level but also at the master's level in social work. So, there is a need for text-book on community organization which can throw the basic concepts, principles etc. in a simple language so that students can have a better and deeper understanding of the method.

The community organization is a method of social work whereby a professional social worker helps individuals, groups, communities or organizations to engage in a planned collective action in order to deal with social problems within a democratic system of values. Ross defined community organization as a process by which a community identifies its needs or objectives, develops the confidence and will to work at these needs or objectives, finds the resources (internal and/ or external) to deal with these needs or objectives, takes action in respect to them, and in so doing extends and develops cooperative and collaborative attitudes and practices in the community.

The book has been organized in to fifteen chapters. The first chapter gives an overview of community organization as a method of social work. It has highlighted the meaning of community organization, basic assumptions; philosophy of community organization, important definitions of community organization as well as purpose of community organization practice etc.The second chapter has discussed the location of Community Work in the context of Social Work. It has provided a brief overview of Community Work and Community organization in Social Work. The third chapter has discussed the history of community organization in UK and USA. The fourth chapter has discussed the history of community organization in India. More importantly it throws some light on the Gandhian concept of community organization. The fourth chapter has discussed the Principles, Values and Ethics of Community Organization Practice and the role of a community organizer in Indian context. The fifth chapter has presented the basic principles of community organization. In the sixth chapter, the values and ethics of community organization has been discussed. The important characteristics and skills of a community organizer are highlighted in the next chapter. The chapter 8 has discussed the role of social worker in community organization practice. The variety of roles performed by community organizer in various settings has been highlighted. The chapter 9 has presented the various models and approaches of community organization. The neighbourhood development model, system change model and structural change model has been discussed. This chapter also describes the various approached of community organization viz. social work approach, political activists approach; neighbourhood maintenance/ community development approach has been elaborated. The basic steps of community organization have been discussed in the next chapter. The chapter 11 has discussed the relevance of community organization for community development. The distinction between community organization and community development has been clearly presented. The chapter 12 has discussed the concept of power and its relevance in the context of community organization. In the next chapter, various current issues of community organization have been covered. The emerging issues like gender sensitive community organization practice, axis of inequality of caste and class have been discussed. In the next chapter, various settings of community organization have been discussed. The last chapter which is an important chapter describes the importance of community organization in managing the conflicts.

The book has been developed keeping in mind the basic requirements of students at the undergraduate and master's level. It is believed that the book will be an essential reading for the BSW and MSW Students and development practioners.

Sheeba Joseph
Bishnu Mohan Dash

Contents

Preface

1. **Meaning, Definition and Basic Assumptions of Community Organization** 1
   Community Organization; Philosophy of Community Organization; Value Assumptions; Community Organization as Macro Method of Practice in Social Work; Community Organization as a Problem Solving Method; Methods and Procedures of Community Organization

2. **Location of Community Work in the Context of Social Work** 14
   Location of Community Work within Social Work; Concept of Community Analysis

3. **History of Community Organization in U.K. and U.S.A.** 21
   Why Should we Study History?; History of Community Organization; The Charity Organization Period 1870-1917; The Rise of Federation 1917 to 1935; Period of Expansion and Professional Development 1935 to Present Time; Community Organization in U.K.

4. **History of Community Organization in India**   27
   Difference Between Community Organization and Community Development; Gandhian Approach to Community Organization

5. **Principles of Community Organization Practice**   31
   Principles of Community Organization

6. **Values and Ethics of Community Organization Practice**   39

7. **Characteristics and Skills of a Good Community Organizer**   45
   Characteristics of a Good Organizer

8. **Role of a Social Worker in Community Organization Practice**   49
   Communicator; Enabler; Animator; Guide; Counselor; Collaborator; Consultant; Innovator; Model; Motivator; Catalyst; Advocate; Facilitator; Mediator; Educator; Levels of Consciousness; Magic Level of Consciousness; Naïve Level of Consciousness; Critical Level of Consciousness; Empowerment

9. **Models and Approaches of Community Organization**   58
   Model; Model of Community Organization by Rothman; Model A – Locality Development; Model B – Social Planning; Model C – Social Action; Models of Rothman; Neighbourhood Development Model; System Change Model; Structural Change Model; Approaches to Community Organization; Neighborhood Organizing; The Social Work Approach; The Political Activists Approach; Neighborhood Maintenance/Community Develop-ment Approach

10. **Basic Steps in Community Organization**   67
    Identifying the Problem; Perception of the Problem - Facts and Data; Structural - Functional Analysis; Beneficiaries Profile; Action Plan; Determination of Strategy; Linking People with the Programme; Implementation and Evaluation; Building Counter System

11. **Relevance of Community Organization in Community Development**   70
    Distinction Between Community Organization and Community Development; Working with Individuals, Families, and Groups with in the Community

12. **Understanding Power in the Context of Community Organization**   75
    Concept of Power; The Dimensions of Power; The Relevance of Power in Community Organization; Barriers of Empowerment

13. **Current Issues in Community Organization**   81
    Gender Sensitive Community Organization Practice; Male-Female Differentiation; Allocation of Roles; Gender-based Hierarchical Placement; Elements of the Gender System; Caste as a Unit and as a System; Axis of Inequality of Caste and Class; Caste; Class

14. **Settings of Community Organization Practice in Social Work**   87
    Social Action; Community Welfare Planning; Principles of Planning; Three Contrary Views; Value Assumptions

15. **Importance of Community Organization Practice in Conflict Resolution**   100
    What is Conflict; Types of Conflict; Conflict and Competition; The Dimensions of Conflict; The Effects of Conflict – Positive Aspects of Conflict; When, Where and Why is Conflict Likely to Occur?; Type of Event or Issue; Type of Local Government; Understanding Conflict as a Strategy in Social Change; Managing Conflict

    Bibliography   121
    Index   *129*

1. Meaning, Definition and Basic Assumptions of Community Organization

The term 'community organization' has several meanings. It is being often used synonymous to community work, community development and community mobilization. In general, community organization means helping the community to solve its problems. In the context of social work profession in India, the term is used to denote a method of social work to intervene in the life of a community. The aim of community organization is 'developing a capacity' in the community 'by making it more organised' to handle its own needs or problems.

In sociology we learn that society and social institutions are more than just a collection of individuals. They include how those individuals are linked to each other. They are sets of systems such as economy, political organization, value, ideas, belief systems, technology, and patterns of expected behaviours (social interaction). It means that just collections of individuals living at a common place are not necessarily organized. To call them organized they needs to have a set of common ideas and expectations. This gives them a social structure and some social processes that make the organization something (social). It goes beyond the very individuals that compose the community.

Further it is important to note that just forming various groups in community having some structure or form (e.g. having a president, treasurer, secretary, etc.) does not make the community organized. It is not the multiplicity of institutions, interest groups or set of activities, which make the organized community, for it, may create more conflicts and disrupt the normal life. Thus the important determining factors of community organization are interaction, integration and co-ordination of the existing institutions, interest groups and activities, and evolving new groups and institutions if necessary to meet the changing conditions and needs of the community.

To study and to be able to engage in community organization practice it is necessary to have a clear definition. There are several definitions available in literature, which are put forth at different times and context. The common element in most of them is matching resources to needs. We will discuss here two most widely accepted definitions of community organization.

Murray G. Ross (1967) defines community organization as a "process by which a community identifies its needs or objectives, gives priority to them, develops the confidence and will to work at them, finds resources (internal and external) to deal with them, and in doing so, extends and develops co-cooperative and collaborative attitudes and practices in the community."

In this definition by "process" he meant a movement from identification of a problem or objective to solution of the problem or attainment of the objective in the community. There are other processes for dealing with community problems, but here he called the community organization process that by which the capacity of the community to function as an integrated unit grows as it deals with one or more community problems. The task of the professional worker in community organization is to help initiate, nourish, and develop this process. His task is also to make this process conscious, deliberative, and understood.

"Community", in the sense in which it is used here, refers to two major groupings of people. Firstly, it may be all the people in a specific geographic area, i.e., a village, a town, a city, a neighbourhood, or a district in a city. In the same manner it could refer also to all the people in a province or a state, a nation, or in the world. Secondly, it is used to include groups of people who share some common interests or functions, such as welfare, agriculture, education, and religion. In this context community organization may be involved in bringing these persons together to develop some awareness of, and feeling for their "community" and to work at common problems arising out of the interest or function they have in common.

The second definition that we discuss here is by Kramer and Specht (1975), which is in more technical terms. They defined that "Community organization refers to various methods of intervention whereby a professional change agent helps a community action system composed of individuals, groups or organizations to engage in planned collective action in order to deal with special problems within the democratic system of values."

According to their explanations it involves two major inter-related concerns:

(a) the interaction process of working with an action system which includes identifying, recruiting and working with the members and developing organizational and interpersonal relationships among them which facilitates their efforts; and

(b) the technical tasks involved in identifying problem areas, analyzing causes, formulating plans, developing strategies and mobilizing the resources necessary to effect action.

Mc Neil (1951) defines "community organization has been defined as the process of bringing about and maintaining a progressively more effective adjustment between social welfare needs within a geographic area or functional field. Its goals are consistent with all social work goals in that its primary focus is upon the needs of people and provisions of means of meeting these needs in a manner consistent with the percepts of democratic living".

Friedlander (1955) defines "Community organization for social welfare may be defined as the social work process of establishing a progressively more effective adjustment between the social welfare needs and the community welfare resources within a geographical area". (Freiedlander, W.A., p. 187.)

Explaining the meaning of "geographic area ", Fiedlander has included in the practice of community organization, community, city, district including other geographical areas like state, country and international area. Adjustment between community resources and social welfare needs is achieved with the help of social workers through community resources and other groups in the community.

As a process community organization for social welfare passes through many stages, i.e.:

1. Knowledge of the structure of the community welfare and social agencies and their functioning.

2. Co-ordination between the available facilities of government and private agencies for providing high level of services.

3. Improvement in the standards of government and private agencies.

4. Use of survey and research for determining the current unmet human needs.

5. Analysis of these needs with reference to available resources.

6. Synthesis of information, examination of facts and deciding priority keeping in view the importance and necessity of needs.

7. Discontinuity of unnecessary services or coordination and development of needed new services.
8. To increase the knowledge of current services before the public and all groups or to interpret the need for the creation of new services.
9. To mobilize financial resources and moral support for social welfare activities; and
10. To create knowledge in the community regarding the need for social welfare through education and information.

United Nations (1955) has recognized community development as one of the most important factors, specially when this concept is used with respect to the economically less developed countries. While clarifying the close relationship between "Community development" and "Community Organization" and explaining that the later concepts is more comprehensive than "community welfare organization", both concepts "community development" and "community organization" are supplementary to each other and has defined these two concepts as follows:

Community development:

> "The term "Community development" is currently used mainly in relation to the rural areas of less –developed countries, whose major embassis is placed upon activities for the improvement of the basic living conditions of the community, including the satisfaction of some of its nonmatieal needs." (United Nations", Principals of Community Development", exempted from social progress through community development (1955).

Community Organization

The term "community organization "covers a series of activities at the community level aimed at bringing about desired improvement in the social well-being of individuals, groups and neighbourhoods". Community organizing is about creating a Democratic instrument to bring about sustained social change. According to Murray G. Ross, "Community organization is a process by which a community identifies needs and takes action, and in doing so . . . develops co-operative attitudes and practices".

Philosophy of Community Organization

The early attempts in community organization were an outcome of the serious problems i.e. problems of unemployment, poverty etc. faced by the communities. Thus grew up many organizations and social agencies to provide support to the community. Soon, it was realized that all these efforts need to be co-ordinated and streamlined so as to avoid duplicity of work and to reduce the gap in the delivery of services to the community. At one point of time we might ask, What has been the driving force behind all these efforts that prompted the people of Good will to render services to the community? Let us look at the philosophy of community Organization, which may throw some light on this theme. The fundamental aspect of the community organizations is the principle of "co-operative spirit" which promotes the people to unite together to address a common issue. Community organization recognizes the spirit of democratic values and principles and community organization is about is creating democratic involvement.

Organizing is about empowering. When people unite together, barring all discriminations and get involved in the community organizations, they develop confidence. This empowerment comes when people learn skills to help themselves and others. The collective action helps in community building. The community organization recognizes the power of individual. It believes, through the collective strength of the people, better teamwork and adopting scientific methods can make comprehensive social problems. Another Philosophy is that of coordination. It is concerned with the adjustments and inter-relations of the forces in the community life for a common welfare. Community organization is therefore, is a continuous process in which adjustments are made and remade to keep pace with the changing conditions of community life.

Harper and *Dunham* have described the objectives of community organization by reffering to those given in its report by Lane Committee constituted by National Conference of Social Work, 1939. The objectives are:

Common Objectives

The common objectives of Community organization as a method is to establish a dynamic and more effective adjustment between social welfare needs and social welfare resources. Common Objectives of Community Organization are:

(a) Defining and finding out the needs(Felt and express).

(b) Preventing of disabilities and rejection of social needs which are unfair.

(c) Clarification of resources and needs and re-adjustment of resources for the fulfillment of changing needs adequately.

Secondary Objectives

In order to fulfil the common objectives community organization tries to fulfil some secondary objectives which are as follows:

(a) To achieve a realistic basis for a sound planning and effort to maintain it.

(b) To start and develop welfare programmes and services, and to modify them so that adjustment is achieved between resources and needs.

(c) To raise the standard of Social work and to increase the effectiveness of individual agencies.

(d) To improve mutual relationship between groups and individuals offering social welfare programmes and service for bringing about coordination between themselves.

(e) To increase awareness and knowledge in the public regarding welfare-related problems, needs and social work, objectives, programmes and methods.

(f) To seek public support and participation in community welfare activities.

According to Mc Neil the goal of community organization are in conformity with the goal of whole social work because focus of attention in it is on the needs according to the principles of democratic life.

1. Analysing community resources available to meet needs.
2. Gaining facts about human needs
3. Synthesis, correlation and testing of facts.
4. Relating facts about needs to facts about available services.
5. Bringing into participation in all phases of the process, individuals and representative of groups concerned.
6. Fostering interaction of attitudes and representative view points with the objective of reaching agreement through mutual understanding.
7. Stimulating citizen interest in social problems and creating motivation for action through participation and education.
8. Determining priorities.
9. Developing and improving standards of service.
10. Identification of gaps of duplication of services.
11. Adjusting or eliminating existing services or developing new services to meet needs.
12. Enhancing community understanding through education.
13. Mobilizing support – Moral and financial.

Community Organization is one of the primary methods of social work. It deals with intervention in the communities to solve the community problems. As a method of social work community organization can solve the problems of many people in the community through their collective involvement. Community organization and community development are inter-related as two sides of the same coin. The community organization includes other methods of social work, that is, group work, and case work. The power structure plays a role in the community organization. The social workers need to know the community power structure to practise community organization method. Community organization method is used for empowering people for their development. The details are provided for social work students to understand and practise community organization effectively.

Value Assumptions

A simple response to these counter-views would be that community organization as it is defined here, doesn't make cooperation an ultimate good, doesn't deny the value of individual effort, doesn't insist that all goals can be achieved only in cooperative work. Similarly it could be said that the particular conception of community organization outlined here has no tolerance for manipulation but it is disposed towards "open covenants openly arrived at". This interpretation of community organization does not imply denial of the validity and value of other approaches to the solution of the problems of community life (e.g., the need for the planning by social scientists, housing, traffic, zoning, and other types of experts) but asserts that the development of "Community" (both geographic and functional), as interpreted here, is essential if the values implicit in the concept of democracy are to be maintained.

Community organization derives from a unique frame of reference, the nature of which may now be examined. The framework takes its special form as a result of:

1. A particular value orientation which stems from traditional religious values which have been expanded to form the basis of social work philosophy.

2. A particular conception of the problems confronting modern man in his community and social life.
3. Certain assumptions that influence method, which derive in part from the value orientation of and in part from experience in social work.

Community Organization as Macro Method of Practice in Social Work

Community organization is considered as a macro method of practice in social work [Arthur E. Fink]. It is used for solving community problems. The term 'Macro' is used because of its ability to involve a large number of people in solving the social problems. Community organization is a macro method because; community organization can be successfully implemented at local level of community, or at State level of community, or at regional level of the community or at very large international level of community. For example, community organization is possible for pollution control at local, State, regional, national and international levels. It is a macro method because; casework deals with only one person, group work deals with limited number of participants. But community organization deals with number of people and so it is called as macro method. For example, poverty cannot be solved by using individual approach like casework as there are many people affected by poverty. Individual approach is not practical due to the magnitude of the problem. We have to use a method, which can help a large number of people. While comparing other methods of social work community organization as macro method is useful for solving social problems like poverty.

Community Organization as a Problem-solving Method

In community organization method the community is the client. Community organization solves the community problems and fulfils the needs of the community. Many of the community problems like social injustice, poverty, inadequate housing, poor nutrition, lack of health, lack of medical services,

Meaning, Definition and Basic Assumptions ...

unemployment, pollution, exploitation, bonded labour system, illicit arrack, dowry, female infanticide, women and children trafficking, drug trafficking etc. can be solved by using community organization method. In problem solving generally we use three basic aspects. They are study, diagnosis, and treatment. The problem has to be studied. For this we have to collect information regarding the problem. From the information collected we have to find out the causes. This is called as diagnosis. Based on the findings, or diagnosis a solution is evolved that is called as treatment. We consider this model as medical model because doctors study the patient find out the causes for illness and based on findings, treatment or medicine is provided. Similar model is used in community organization method. Problems are solved with involvement of people. The resources are mobilized to solve the problems. This method is applicable for Indian situations because in India a large number of people are affected by poverty or other poverty related problems. They need solutions. For this community organization as a problem solving method can solve community problems. For example people in the dry area suffer due to lack of water for their cultivation. With the help of the community organizer and people's participation watersheds can be made and ground water level is increased. Water stored during rainy season can help the people to continue cultivation. Here the whole village problem is related with water for irrigation and drinking purpose, which is solved by using community organization method.

Community organization method is used for the following:

(a) To meet the needs and bring about and maintain adjustment between needs and resources in a community.

(b) Helping people effectively with their problems and objectives by helping them to develop, strengthen, and maintain qualities of participation, self-direction and cooperation.

(c) Bringing about changes in community and group relationships and in the distribution of decision-making power.

(d) The resources of the community are identified and tapped for solving the community problems.

Methods and Procedures of Community Organization

The objectives of community organization are fulfilled through agencies which function in the community and perform a number of special types of activities. An activity and a method can be differentiated in these words: an activity is a special project or service which takes place as result of the use of a method. An activity is what action is done i.e. a thing which is done and a method is a way through which an activity is performed. In this context Lane has described the following methods used in community organization.

- Continuous centralized records
- Planning
- Special study or Survey
- Joint Budget or Financial system
- Education in community organization process and public contact and relations
- Planning for fund raising, joint campaigns as a method of community organization process.
- Use of methods of community organization
- Area-wise services or any other method of inter-agency consultations.
- Development and use of group discussion and conference method
- Encouraging discussion for merger of two agencies.
- Providing services jointly
- Encouraging social legislation through the applications of social action method.

McNeil has described the following procedures of community organization:
- Administration and process records.
- Research.
- Consultation.
- Group conference.
- Committee operation.
- Interpretation.
- Administration.
- Mobilization of resources.
- Negotiation.

These processes and methods will be used in different situations when a person works in the community. A description of these processes in human relationships of community development has been given by UN - Training for social work - Third International Survey in the following manner:

1. Getting to know the local community and winning its acceptance.
2. Gathering knowledge about the local community - size of the universe, sex, age, occupation, economic status, etc.
3. Identifying the local leader.
4. Stimulating the community to realize about their problems.
5. Helping people to identifying the pressing problems and to discuss their problems.
6. Fostering Self-confidence.
7. Deciding on a programme of action.
8. Recognition of strengths and resources.
9. Helping the people to continue to work on solving their problems.
10. Increasing people's ability for self-help.

2. Location of Community Work in the Context of Social Work

Having discussed the meaning and definition of community organization lets now try to situate it in the context of community work and social work profession. In social work the term "community work" is often used with different meanings. In social work literature we find that the term "community work", "community development", "community organization" and "community empowerment" are at times inter-changeably used for the work with communities. Some authors have used these terms for the same type of work whereas others use them to refer to different type of work with communities.

Community work has a long history as an aspect of social work. It has passed through various phases. All over the world it has been recognized as an integral part of social work practice. History shows that community work even preceded social work education. In U.K. and U.S.A. community work in social work began in the 1800 with the charity organization movement and the settlement house movement. During the initial phase in U.K. community work was primarily seen as a method of social work, trying to help individuals to enhance their social adjustment. The main thrust was to act as a means to coordinate the work of voluntary agencies.

In India the experience of working with slum community in the city of Bombay lead to the establishment of the first institution of social work education in 1937. Community work as a method of social work in India is largely seen as a process of developing local initiatives, particularly in the areas of education, health and agriculture development. The focus of the work is, to encourage people to express their needs, and enable them to avail the existing resources.

There are several ways in which social work practitioners and others work in the community. In social work we find three main approaches namely, community development, community organization and community relations/services. While these approaches represent different situations or areas of community work there are fundamental similarities in what is being attempted. Their components are often inter-linked and at times overlapping.

What is important for us here to understand is that the community work is one of the basic social work processes. It is being used to attain the same basic objectives, as casework and groupwork. As you may be aware that all the social work methods are concerned with removal of the blocks to growth of individual, group, or community, release of their potentialities, full use of inner resources, development of capacity to manage one's own life and their ability to function as an integrated unit. In community organization particularly, social work is concerned with the initiation of that process which enable a community to overcome those blocks (apathy, vested interests, discrimination) which prevent the community from working together; release of potentialities and use of indigenous resources and growth of those cooperative attitude and skills which make possible achievement of increasingly difficult ends.

Thus, community organization is more of a product of the maturation process than of the beginnings of the profession. The increasingly complex and inter-dependent nature of modern society makes community organization almost a pre-requisite for reasonably smooth functioning.

Location of Community Work within Social Work

We know that social work profession has three main methods case work, group work and community work/organization are the three main methods and social action, social research are the three ancillary methods. As we know social work profession came in practice round about world war and gradually developed to its present form. Community work/organization term was first used in America before the First World War and was included in social work curriculam there as a subject in 1940. Community work begun in England with organization charity to assist needy poor through settlement houses. It came in practice in third world countries for developmental programmes in the middle of 20th century and now being used as a well established professional method of helping people. It has achieved a fully recognised and well accepted status of a method of social work in social work curriculam as well as social work practice in developed nation and under developed wherever social work is taught and practised.

The exact location of community work within social work is neither possible nor necessary to have a consensus as it depends on the need, demand, requirement, resource, facility, willingness, feasibility, circumstances and nature of the clientele to be served helped that which medhod of social work practice will suit most in that situation to solve the referred or diagnosed problem. History of evolution of methods of social work locate community work at third place. First of all, case work came in practice and later to that community work came in practice but the energence of these three methods happened with slight timing differences and thus that may be treated as insignificant and may be ignored. In developed countries case work and after that group work methods are more popular and in wide practice but in developing and under developed countries of third world, community work is more prominent. An overall picture of social work profession and practice locates community, work organization approximately in its middle position. It does not mean that in any way it has less significance or importance to any other method of social work, rather soldier and incorporate in addition, responsibility and task of other main methods of social work in many ways.

Concept of Community Analysis

Structure and Function: It is a prerequisite to any profession to know the nature it's client. In medical profession before prescribing medicine to the patient doctor has to know about the nature of the patient, his dieting preferences and willingness of intake of medicine etc. Before constructing a bridge on the river, the nature of it's flow of water and highest level during flood should be priorly known to the engineer for preventive measures. To know the nature of the clientele we analyse that in it's various components having different traists. Becoming aware of different traits it becomes easy to formulate remedies for the clientele. The basis of the concept of community analysis is the same. To be successful in community organization/work it is essential to analyse the community being adopted for help.

Community organization thinkers and practitioners have divided components of community in two categories i.e.

1. Horizontal; and
2. Vertical.

Horizontal Components

Horizontal components are structural and functional relationships between various social institution, systems and forces within the communities are structural and functional relationships with out side the community. Analysing various horizontal components of the community worker should to be into consideration:

1. Background and setting
2. History, geography
3. Demography

4. Transportation communication
5. Economic life
6. Government, politics, law enforcement
7. Housing
8. Education
9. Recreation
10. Religion
11. Health and Sanitation
12. Associations, Agencies and unions
13. Ecology and environment; and
14. Social institutions like, caste, religion, family etc.

The community should be aware about the total areas of the community, its origin, evolution and development, location and cultural foundation, roads, lanes, traditional and modern means of transportation like bullock-carts, tractors, cycles, rickshaw, jeeps etc. Population structure including total population and its age, sex, caste, race, ethnicity based distributions, facilities of telephone, television, postal services, cinema, theatre, cellular phones, newspapers etc., occupations like agriculture, horticulture, fishery, dairy, animal husbandry, cottage industry and per capita income etc., facilities of development block, police substation, political parties, leaders and institutions like village panchayat, nyaya panchayat, development area committee, mandi samiti, school and tutorial/coaching centres, vocational training centres, residential facilities, accommodations, night shelters, playgrounds, clubs, playing materials, temples/worshipping places, hospitals, health centres, doctors, nurses, sanitation, drinking water, maximum/minimum and normal tempereture, rivers, wells, ponds, plantation, rainfalls, mountains, plateau, soil etc.; labour unions, welfare and other agencies, living pattern and facilities, social/economic and political institutions, etc. Apart from these the worker should take into consideration the pattern and quality positive attitude, value and ethics related with assimilation, cooperation, initiation, leadership, interaction, response, willingness, acceptance, harmony, participation etc. and negative attitudes like communal, racial or caste feeling destruction, apathy, political rewaley, class feeling and their interrelationship etc.; individuals groups, organizations and agencies within or outside the community having influence on the community to be helped through community work.

Vertical Components

To analyse vertical components of the community, a community organiser/worker should be aware of all those resources which influence the community and its functioning from outside the community. These resources may be either federal or state government and their agencies, laws officials etc. or International, quasi-governmental or voluntary agencies or organizations, their personnel, officers, laws, schemes, programmes etc. These resources may have influence or involvement in activities in a community considering that as their primary unit of operation.

Whether the component is horizontal or vertical the community organiser/worker should know its collective structure and function both. They should be aware of setting of each component in its particular special pattern with specific relation to each other. They should also be familiar with functions of each and every component whether that is assisting, cooperating, assimilating, or disturbing, disintegrating or opposing to the community work. Keeping into consideration the above analytical elements in the beginning and planning for the community work, the worker may proceed smoothly and get adequate fruitful results. Community analysis helps mobilizing resources within and outside the community, utilizing them in the best suitable way and strengthening harmonious relationship between individuals, groups, sub systems, agencies, personnel and officials etc.

The main values of community organization are dignity, self-respect, equal opportunity, liberty, tolerence, democracy, constructive cooperation.

The ethics of community organization are maintenance of high standard of personal conduct, competence in professinal practice, regard for profession, adoption of undated methods of enquiry and research, service with devotion and loyalty, maintenance and protection of confidentiality, colleagues respect, and action for prevention and elimination of discrimination.

Exact location of community work within social work is neither possible nor necessary. History of evolution of methods of social work locates community work at third place. An overall picture of social work profession locates community work in its middle position. Authors have divided the nature of community in two categories i.e.:

1. Horizontal; and
2. Vertical for community analysis.

The horizontal nature includes structural and functional relationships of various social components and systems in the community. The vertical nature includes structured and functional relationships of its components of sources outside the community.

As you are already aware that, It has been practiced as a method of social work in the western countries; especially in England and U.S.A. However, little has been written about the history of community organization. Community organization is a process and is all about solving the present day today problems of common interests by way of adopting democratic principles and peoples participation. People have used this method in the past and have attained desired results. Thus, it is important for the students of community organization to understand the past, draw lessons from it and develop and experiment new models and methods required to work with community.

3. History of Community Organization in U.K. and U.S.A.

Here, we will be dealing with the history of community organization in England, USA and provide you with a brief idea about the community organization practice in India. In the later part of the chapter, we will also discuss some of the models and approaches of community organization.

Why Should we Study History?

We can learn a lot from the history, that variety of social-change groups faced with long odds and with slim beginnings won out in the end. History makes us clear that slow times need not mean the death of hope. But lends us patience while teaching us persistence. The strategies adopted in the past provide us concrete lessons on tactics and approaches allowing each generation to build on the knowledge of its predecessors. It is all about the problems the people experienced and the solution they achieved. In short, history sensitizes us to the problems and possibilities of change, provides concrete advice for the present-day action, and sustain our action with the hope and pride that comes from learning of past experience. Therefore, the study of the history of community organization becomes essential for a social worker.

History of Community Organization

In a broad sense we can say wherever people have lived together, some form of organizations has emerged. These informal associations of people always tried to do good to the people in need and protect the rights of the society. On the contrary the history talks about the formal organizations which were set up for the welfare of the community. The first efforts at community organization for social welfare were initiated in England to overcome the acute problem of poverty, which led to beggary.

The first effort of its kind was the Elizabethan poor law (1601) in England, which was set up to provide services to the needy. Another important landmark in the history of community organization is the formation of London Society of organizing charitable relief and repressing mendicancy and the origin of the settlement house movement in England during 1880.

In fact, these movements had a major impact in the United States of America. In 1880 the charities organization was set up to put rational order in the area of charity and relief. The major community organization activities in the United States could be classified into three periods:

The Charity Organization Period 1870-1917

This era is the beginnings in social welfare in U.S.A. The first citywide Charity Organization Society (COS) was established in the Buffalo in 1877 in U.S.A. This movement was started with the influence of London Charity Organization established in 1869. In U.S.A., Rev. S.H. Gurteen, an English priest who had an association with London Charity Association and had moved to Buffalo in 1873 gave the leadership to this movement. With in a short span of six years the COS had reached to more than 25 American cities.

Charity organization was concerned about two things:

- Providing adequate personal services to families and individuals in need
- Take steps to address the issues/problems in social welfare.

Apart from these services the COS also took initiatives in promoting co-operation among the various welfare agencies. From this movement of charity organization emerged many other such service-oriented organizations i.e. Social Service Exchange, Community Welfare Councils, Councils of Social Agencies.

The Rise of Federation (1917 to 1935)

It is a period where we can see the growth and development of chests and councils. It started with the rise of war chests in 1917 and ended with the enactment of social security act, which set the stage for development of the public welfare programs in 1935. A large number of chests and councils came up after World War I. The American Association for Community Organization (AACO) was organized in 1918 as the national agency for chests and councils and it later became known as Community Chests and Councils of (CCC) America. The Cincinnati Public Health Federation, established in 1917 was the first independent health council in American city. It is in this period that the American Association of Social Workers organized in 1921, the first general professional organization, set up its training for the social workers and others who specialized in community organization.

A community chest is a voluntary welfare agency, co-operative organization of citizens and welfare agencies, which is the powerful local force for community welfare origination that handles large funds. It has two functions. It raises funds through a community-wide appeal and distributes them according to a systematic budget procedure. Secondly, it promotes co-operative planning, co-ordination and administration of the communities social welfare.

Period of Expansion and Professional Development from 1935 to Present Time

It is in this period the we see the greater use of the community organization process in the filed of public welfare. A marked significance of this era is the establishment of Federal Security Agency where we see the maximized involvement of the government in welfare programmes. In 1946 the agency was strengthened and re-organized following which in 1953 Department of Health, Education and Welfare was established.

Another important factor of the period is about the professional development that took place. Some of the important professional developments are:

The National Conference of Social Work in 1938-39 undertook a study on community organization, which later publicized the nature of "Generic Community Welfare Organization". Based on this another study took place in 1940, but due to America involvement in World War II an active programme could not take off.

In 1946, at the National Conference of Social Work in Buffalo, the Association of the Study of Community Organization (ASCO) was organized. The main objective was to improve the professional practice of organization for social welfare. In 1955, ASCO merged with six other professional organizations to form the National Association of Social Workers. Community organization has been recognized as integral and important aspect of social work education in the American Association of Schools of Social Work Education. At present there is an active committee of Council on Social Work education involved in the production of teaching materials in community organization.

The first contemporary textbook on community organization titled "Community Organization for Social Welfare" published in 1945 has been written by Wayne McMilen.

Another development in the history of community development is seen in the wake of World War II. Wartime needs were very special and crucial. During this time many councils and community war services came to the forefront. Among them United Service Organization (USO) is of prime importance as it was the union of many forces that served the needs of the military personnel and defence communities. The other striking characteristics of the period is the immense increase in the volunteer service i.e. defence council, American Red Cross and USO which co-ordinated and recruited the volunteers.

Another development that took place at the wartime is the growth of closer relationship between labour and social work, which is considered as great significance to community origination.

The other developments that took place after the World War II are as follows that are very specific to community organization area as follows:

- The rehabilitation of the physically and mentally challenged.
- Mental health planning, problems of the aging.
- Prevention and treatment of juvenile delinquency.

In order to address theses issues separate bodies were set up and we see the entry of international agencies in the field of community origination. The present situation in community organization is the emergence of the new community development programs, which aims at providing, services to the less developed areas in the international social welfare. Therefore the present agenda is on working with the whole community and a greater emphasis on self-help.

Community Organization in U.K.

Baldock (1974) has summed up the historical development in U.K. by diving it in to four phases.

The First Phase

1880-1920: During this period the community work was mainly seen as a method of social work. It was considered as a process of helping the individuals to enhance their social adjustments. It acted as major player to co-ordinate the work of voluntary agencies.

The Second Phase

1920-1950: This period saw the emergence of new ways of dealing with social issues and problems. The community organization was closely associated with central and state Government programme for urban development. The important development in this period was its association with community association movement.

The Third Phase 1950 Onwards

It emerged as a reaction to the neighbourhood idea, which provided an ideological phase for the second phase. It was period we see the professional development of social work. Most of the educators and planners tried to analyze the shortcomings in the existing system. It was also a period where the social workers sought for a professional identity.

The Fourth Phase

It is a period that has marked the involvement of the community action. It questioned the very relationship of the community work and social work. It was thus seen as period of radical social movement and we could see the conflicts of community with authority. The association of social workers and the community were de-professionalized during this period. Thus, it was during this period the conflictual strategies that were introduced in the community work, although even now there is no consensus on this issue (Baldock, 1974).

History of Community Organization in India

A historical account of the community organization is not available in India, as there has been only a rare documentation on social work literature in general and community organization in particular. Community organization has its roots in the charity organizations in the United States. They realized the need of the people and tied to organize the people to coordinate their work. The main activities were social welfare, raising funds, seeking enactment for the social legislation and co-ordination of welfare activities. The spirit behind all these activities was charity. In India, the very concept of charity is deep rooted in the religious philosophy. Even before the commencement of the social work education in India in 1937, the community work was in place. But in the first phase from 1937 to 1952 the community work was in a dormant stage. During this period the social work was in its infancy and not many were employed in the community settings because. There were hardly any jobs that provided an opening for community organization. Professionals preferred to work in casework settings.

It was in 1952 the community development project was launched in India and with this we find the emergence of a new era of community work. The basic objective of community development in India was to awaken the rural people of their needs, instilling in them a sense of ambition for better life and making them aware of their right and power to find a solution for their problems. According to Mukerji (1961) "Community development is a movement designed to promote better living for the whole community with the active participation and if possible with the initiative of community". According to him community development can be divided in to two process.

1. Extension education; and
2. Community organization.

Extension education was expected to improve the quality of human beings by improving his/her knowledge and skills. By community organization Mukerji had in mind the setting up of the following three institutions in the village:

1. Village Panchayat;
2. Village co-operative; and
3. Village school.

During this period the thrust of the community work remained rural where as social work remained urban in character.

From 1970 onwards we could see a new trend in the community work practice. The social workers expanded their scope and operational area from their traditional approach of casework to other developments fields. For example people working with school children started working with the community. The NGOs and voluntary organization adopted a community approach. This shift has in-fact led to the use of process of community work. By and large the community work has remained welfare-oriented.

The current phase of community work in India is experiencing a growing dissatisfaction with its own practice or rather the outcome of its practice. So efforts are on to create alternate ways of working with communities. In-spite of these, the professionals is involved in a variety of projects in both rural and urban areas to promote better living for the community.

Another trend in the community work is the involvement of the Business houses in promoting welfare in their neighborhood. This is commonly known as CSR (Corporate social responsibilities) The business houses i.e. Tatas, Escorts, and some of the multinational companies too have joined in this venture. This trend has attracted many professionals in this field

The main objective of community development is to develop village communities by methods, which will stimulate, encourage and aid villagers themselves to do much of the work necessary to accomplish the desired goals. The changes conceived and promoted should have the involvement of the people and should be acceptable to them and put in to practice by them.

Difference Between Community Organization (CO) and Community Development (CD)

There is a common philosophical base between community organization and community development. Both aims to enable people to live happily and fully developed life. Both have basic faith in the common man and his right to self-determination in the framework of the society. Both give emphasis to self-help and help the people to help themselves to solve their own problems. However, community organization and community development should not be considered as synonymous:

1. The CD is concerned with the promotion of all aspects of life including social, economical and cultural; both in rural and urban areas. While CO is concerned with adjustment of social welfare needs and resources in cities, states, Nations as well as in villages.
2. The CO is practiced in the U.S.A. on a voluntary basis. While CD in almost all the developing countries are a government-sponsored programme.

3. The CO is a product of urbanization and industrialization. Here the main concern is problems of the population mobility, problems of the family, problems of the aged, problems of the juvenile delinquency, of unemployment and provision of social security. But CD is concerned with how to induce people to meet their basic human needs.
4. The CO tends to be more process oriented while CD as practiced in India tends to be target oriented.

Gandhian Approach to Community Organization

Gandhi has not given a literary definition of the term community. For him the village is the basic community with geographical limitation where a number of families come together and co-operate to build a common life. According to Gandhi the basic element of a community is mutual co-operation and common sharing. The emphasis of Gandhian concept of community organization is the reconstruction of the community rather than on organizing of an unorganized or disorganized community or on the development of entirely a new community.

Therefore the Gandhian objective of community organization is to reconstruct the village communities spread all over the country. This construction is based on the 19 item constructive programme designed to meet the social welfare needs of the community. It is through the construction of the village community Gandhi aims to realize he goal of reconstructing the "sarvodaya Social order".

Gandhi has not given any specific or fixed pattern for the reconstruction programme but left it to the capacity of those community organizers and to suit to the different conditions and social situations. The role of the worker in this approach is very distinct. Here, the worker not only deals with those groups of people or communities who seek his guidance but also would approach those communities, which do not ask for help as his prime work being the reconstruction of the society. In this approach the worker takes initiatives and gradually stimulates the community .It demands the regularity and sincerity of the worker in the reconstruction programme.

5 Principles of Community Organization Practice

We understand that community organization is an integral part of social work practice. In order to practice community organization some obvious questions arise that how should it be done? Are there any value orientations and general principles that may guide us in deciding what is sound or good or socially desirable community organization? What is desirable or accepted in community organization practice? How to improve the chances of success in achieving the objectives of community organization? We deal with these and such other questions in this section.

Community organization derives from a unique frame of reference, the nature of which is based on a particular value orientation. In social work, the focus of community organization practice is influenced by a system of personal and professional values. These values affects workers style of intervention and the skills they use in working with community members. Values are beliefs that delineate preferences about how one ought or ought not to behave. Such formulations of values obviously have a large subjective element. Values differ between groups and between individuals within the same group. Moreover, there has been no explicit, comprehensive, or generally accepted formulation of basic ethical and social values by any representative group of community organization practitioners.

Principles of Community Organization

Principles of community organization, in the sense in which the term is used here are generalized guiding rules for the sound practice. Principles are expressions of value judgements. The principles of community organization, which are being discussed here, are within the frame of and in harmony with the spirit and purpose of social work in a democratic society. We are concerned with the dignity and worth, the freedom, the security, the participation, and the wholesome and abundant life of every individual. This implies following the principles of democracy, involvement of the marginalized, transparency, honesty, sustainability, self-reliance, partnerships, cooperation, etc.

In the literature of community organization we find various sets of principles. Dunham (1958) has presented a statement of 28 suggested principles of community organization. He grouped those under the following seven headings:

1. Democracy and social welfare.
2. Community roots for community programmes.
3. Citizen understanding, support, and participation and professional service.
4. Co operation.
5. Social welfare programmes.
6. Adequacy, distribution, and organization of social welfare services.
7. Prevention.

Ross (1967) outlined specific principles – the elementary or fundamental ideas regarding initiation and continuation of community organization processes. These principles have been discussed in terms of the nature of the organization or association and the role of the professional worker. The twelve principles identified by Ross are:

Principles of Community Organization Practice

1. Discontent with existing conditions in the community must initiate and/or nourish development of the association.
2. Discontent must be focused and channelled into organization, planning, and action in respect to specific problems.
3. Discontent which initiates or sustains community organization must be widely shared in the community.
4. The association must involve leaders (both formal and informal) identified with, and accepted by major sub-groups in the community.
5. The association must have goals and methods and procedures of high acceptability.
6. The programme of the association should include some activities with an emotional content.
7. The association should seek to utilize the manifest and latent goodwill which exists in the community.
8. The association must develop active and effective lines of communication both within the association and between the association and the community.
9. The association should seek to support and strengthen groups which it brings together in cooperative work.
10. The association should develop a pace of work relative to existing conditions in the community.
11. The association should seek to develop effective leaders.
12. The association must develop strength, stability and prestige in the community.

Keeping in mind the actual practice situations in India Siddiqui (1997) have worked out a set of eight principles:

1. The principle of specific objectives.
2. The principle of planning.
3. The principle of people's participation.

4. The principle of inter-group approach.
5. The principle of democratic functioning.
6. The principle of flexible organization.
7. The principle of optimum utilisation of indigenous resources.
8. The principle of cultural orientation.

We are trying to interpret some of the principles from the available sets of principles for guiding our practice of community organization in Indian context.

1. **Community organization is means and not an end:** As discussed earlier the community organization is a process by which the capacity of the community to function as an integrated unit is being enhanced. In this sense it is a method or a means to enable people to live a happy and fully developed life. It refers to a method of intervention whereby a community consisting of individuals, groups or organizations are helped to engage in planned collective action in order to deal with their needs and problems.

2. **Community organization is to promote community solidarity and the practice of democracy:** It should seek to overcome disruptive influences, which threaten the well-being of the community and the vitality of democratic institutions. In community organization discrimination and segregation or exclusion should be avoided and integration and mutual acceptance should be promoted.

3. **The clear identification of the community:** Since the community is the client of the community organization worker, it must be clearly identified. It is likely that there are several communities with which he/she deals at the same time. Further it is important that once the community is identified the entire community must be the concern of the practitioner. No programme can be isolated from the social welfare needs and resources of the community

Principles of Community Organization Practice 35

as a whole. The welfare of the whole community is always more important than the interest or the well being of any one agency/group in the community.

4. **Fact-finding and needs assessment:** Community organization programmes should have its roots in the community. Proper fact-finding and assessment of the community needs is the pre-requisite for starting any programme in the community. It is generally desirable for local community services to be indigenous, grass-roots developments rather than to be imposed form without. Whenever possible, then, a community organization should have its origin in a need felt by the community or by some substantial number of persons in the community and there should be vital community participation, and usually essential community control, in its development.

    While facilitating the process of community organization the programmes should be initiated, developed, modified, and terminated on the basis of the needs of the community and on the basis of the availability of other comparable services. When the particular need for a service is met, the programme should be modified or terminated.

5. **Identification, mobilization and utilization of the available resources:** The fullest possible use should be made of existing social welfare resources, before creating new resources or services. In the absence of resources/services the worker has to mobilize the resources from various sources such as community, government, non-government agencies, etc. While utilizing the indigenous resources it must be recognised that these resources may sometimes need extensive overhauling before they will meet certain needs. Apart from mobilizing physical resources, indigenous human resources should be put to optimum use.

6. **Participatory planning:** The community organization worker must accept the need for participatory planning

throughout the process of community organization. It is important that the practitioner prepares a blue print in the beginning of what he/she intends to do with the community. This is done with the community taking into consideration the needs of the community, available resources, agency objectives, etc. Planning in community organization is a continuous process as it follows the cycle of implementation and evaluation. The planning should be on the basis of ascertained facts, rather than an expression of guesswork, "hunches", or mere trial and error.

In order to foster the greater participation it is necessary to analyse the impeding factors and take timely steps to remove them. Instead of forcing people to participate in all the issues they should be encouraged to participate at a level and issues in accordance with their capacities. It must be noted that the people will participate if they are convinced of the benefits of the programme.

7. **Active and vital participation:** The concept of self-help is a core of community organization. The community members' participation throughout the process of community organization should be encouraged from the standpoint both of democratic principle and of feasibility - that is, the direct involvement in the progrmme of those who have the primary stake in it's results. "Self-help" by citizen or clientele groups should be encouraged and fostered.

8. **Communities' right of self determination should be respected:** The role of the community organization worker is to provide professional skill, assistance, and creative leadership in enabling peoples' groups and organizations to achieve social welfare objectives. The community members should make basic decisions regarding programme and policy. While the community organization worker plays a variety of roles in different situations, he is basically concerned with enabling peoples' expression

Principles of Community Organization Practice

and leadership to achieve community organization goals, and not with control, domination, or manipulation.

9. **Voluntary cooperation:** Community organization must be based upon mutual understanding, voluntary acceptance, and mutual agreement. Community organization, if it is to be in harmony with democratic principles, cannot be regimentation; it should not be imposed from outside, but must be derived from the inner freedom and will to unite of those who practice it.

10. **The spirit of cooperation rather than competition, and the practice of coordination of effort**: Community organization practice should be based on the spirit of cooperation rather than competition. The community organization practice has proved that the most effective advances are made through cooperative effort. It is by the coordinated and sustained programmes attacking major problems rather than through sporadic efforts by various groups.

    The emphasis on collaborative and cooperative attitudes and practices does not imply elimination of differences, of tension, or of conflict. In fact we have to recognize that these later forces gives life and vitality to a movement. It must be understood that such conflict can be disruptive and destructive, or it can be positive and creative. What is important for the community organization worker is that he/she identifies such forces and appropriately modifies them to the end beneficial to community as whole.

11. **Recognition and involvement of indigenous leadership:** Community organization as it has been described requires the participation of the people of a community. However, everyone in the community cannot be involved in face-to-face contact with all others in the community; therefore it is important to identify and recognize the leaders (both the formal and informal)

accepted by various groups and subgroups in the community. Inclusion of the respected and accepted leaders with whom the major subgroups identify provides a major step in integrating the community and makes possible initiation of a process of communication which, if it becomes effective, will nourish and sustain the process of community organization.

12. **Limited use of authority or compulsion:** Invoking the application of authority or compulsion may sometimes be necessary in community organization; but it should be used as little as possible, for as short a time as possible, and only as a last resort. When compulsion must be applied, it should be followed as soon as possible by resumption of the cooperative process.

13. **The dynamic and flexible nature of programmes and services:** This principle is basic to sound community organization. Social welfare agencies and programmes must be responsive to the changing conditions, problems, and needs of community life. Community is a dynamic phenomenon, which constantly changes and thus the needs and problems also keeps changing. Therefore, it is necessary that the programmes and services are flexible enough.

14. **Continual participatory evaluation:** As programmes are developed to meet community needs, some time must be set aside for evaluation of the process. Regular feedback from the community is important. Criteria must be set up for evaluation of the programmes, to see how effective the action has been and what has been accomplished.

6. Values and Ethics of Community Organization Practice

Now we would try to understand values and ethics of community organization practice. Here we have to keep two things in mind. The first one is that the values and ethics of social work profession in general, and values and ethics of community organization practice are, more or less, the same community organization method is operative only within the broader frame work of social. The other thing is that the principles and values are very often so much intermingled that it becomes very difficult to separate them values provide base for developing principles. Values direct our thinking and action towards socially accepted patterns.

Different social work thinkers and practitioners have described social work values with different names and have put them under different categories. In this regard quite often Kohs, Herbet Bisno, Konopka, Friedlander, Goldsmith, Hoselitz, Hock, Frank, Green, Hobbes, Inkeles, Royce and Deutsch are being quoted. Here we will take up few significant values commonly applicable to community organization practice.

1. First of all we may take up the worth, dignity, integrily, self-respect, equal opportunity and potentiality of

members of the community. In community work these should be given due place and honour.

2. Next to this we may take up liberty and tolerance. Community should be given full liberty in decision-making and in that process coming differences should be tolerated.

3. Constructive cooperation and coordination are essential for community work and these should be observed not only among individuals of the community but between all members, all agencies and other influencing bodies and persons related with the community.

4. Due place should be given to human stresses, motivations and learning in community work.

5. Approach to community work should be democratic, welfare oriented and need based.

6. Community organization believes in individuals and social change and evolution alongwith their rigidity towards cultural demands.

7. Each person, group or community is some what dependant on other and interdependence is essential for life and progress.

8. Individual is an indireate component of the society and it's needs are specific and common both. Individual and society both have certain responsibility for each other. A community workers has to keep in mind these facts and provide adedquate oppotunities for their progress and development.

9. Community organization practice believes in confidetiality, social justice and modernisation.

After becoming familiar with values of community organization practice we should also be aware of ethicss of community organization.

1. The community organiser should maintain high standards of persosnal conduct as a community worker. The

community organiser should not participate in or be associated with dishonesty, fraud or misrepresentation. He should clearly distinguish between statements and actions made as a private individual and as a representative of community work profession.

2. The community worker should make effort to become and remain competant in professional practice and performance. He should accept responsibilities on the ground of existing proficiency and intention to acquire required competence. He should not misrepresent professional qualifications, education and experience.

3. Community worker should regard the service obligation of the profession. He should retain responsibility for the quality of the service that one assumes, assigns or performs. He should act to prevent inhumane and dishonest practices against any individual, group or community.

4. The community worker should act in accordance with the high level of professional impartiality and integrity. He should be alert and resist the pressures and influences that interfere with professional decision and judgement. He should not exploit professional relationships for personal gain.

5. The community worker engaged in study and research should follow the updated methodss of inquiry. He should carefully consider its consequences for the community and its members and as certain that the research evaluation or inquiry is valuntary and priorly known to them. It should also be kept in mind that information should be confidential and dignified. There should not be any harassment in case of refusal to participation. Community work researcher should also protect participants from physical or mental discomforts, stresses, harm, danger or deprivation. During evaluation work, he should discuss issues only for professional purposes and with persons directly and professionaly

related with them. Community work researcher should take credit only for his actual research work and new findings.

6. The community worker's primary responsibility is community well-being. He should serve his clientele with devotion, loyalty, determination and maximum feasible application of professional skill and competance. He should not exploit relationship for personal gain or use agency for private practice. Community worker's practice should be indiscriminatory in respect of race, colour, sex, age, religion, nationality, marital, status, political belief, physical, mental capability or any other characteristic, status or condition. He should avoid relationships or commitments that contrary to the interest of the community. He should not involve himself in any sexual affair with the client. He should make accurate and complete information available to the community and should apprise community of its rights, risks, opportunities and obligations associated with the services for them. In the interest of the community he should seek advice and consultation with colleagues and supervisors in the interest of the community. The community worker should terminate his services when they are no more required and it should be notified to the community in time and further action in relation to the community needs should be pointed out.

7. The community worker should make or efforts to maximise self determination. The community worker should safegaurd the interest and rights of the community members and he should not be engaged in any action violating or diminishing civil or legal rights of the persons related with his activities and programmes.

8. The community worker should take due care regarding maintenance and protection of confidentiality pertaining to the obtained informations, their recording, taping and permitting for other's observation.

Values and Ethics of Community Organization Practice

9. In case of setting fees for any service to the community, the community worker should ensure that they are reasonable, considerate and fair and in accordance with the ability to pay. He should not accept any thing for referral service.

10. A community worker should treat colleagues with respect, courtesy, fairness and good faith. He should cooperate with colleagues and seek arbitration when conflicts with colleagues require resolution.

11. The community worker has the responsibility to relate with others with full professional consideration. The worker to serves the client or colleagues during their emergency.

12. The community worker should be responsible and abide himself to the committments made to the employing organization. He should work to improve policies, procedures, efficiency and effectiveness of the services of employing agency. He should act to prevent and eliminate discrimination in the employees and employers and in its employment policies and practices.

13. Community worker should maintain integrity of the profession and should uphold and enhance the values, ethics, knowledge and mission of the profession. He should take action to proper channel against unethical conduct by any other member of the profession. He should also act to prevent the unauthorised and unqualified practice of community work.

14. The community worker should assist the profession in making social services available to the mass in general. He should have spare time and professional expertise to activate that promote respect for the utility, the integrity and the competence of profession. He should support the formulation, development, enactment and implementation of social policies related to the profession.

15. The community worker should take responsibility for identifying, developing and utilizing knowledge for

professional practice of community work. He should critically examine the emerging knowlege relevant to community work and contribute to the knowledge base and share knowledge and practice with coworkers.

16. The community worker should promote the general welfare of the community as well as the society. He should act to prevent and eliminate descrimination against any person or group on the basis of race or sex, religion or nationality, age or marital status, political belief or personal characteristics or condition or status. He should be aware and ensure that all community members have adequate resources, services and opportunities they require. He should also act to expand opportunity for disadvantaged or oppressed groups and persons.

7. Characteristics and Skills of a Good Community Organizer

Characteristics of a Good Organizer

1. **Curiosity** – The function of an organizer is to raise questions that agitate, that break through the accepted pattern. He goes forth with the questions and suspects that there are no answers but only further questions.

2. **Irreverence** – Curiosity and irreverence go together. He is challenging, insulting, agitating, discrediting. He stirs unrest. In other words creating the discontentment among the people by high lighting the situation or making the people to understand the situation.

3. **Imagination** – To the organizer, imagination is not only a mental creation but something deeper. It ignites and feeds the force that drives him to organize for change. To realistically appraise and anticipate the probable reactions of the resisting forces, he must be able to identify with them too, in his imagination and foresee their reactions to his action.

4. **A Sense of Humour** – Humour is essential to successful tactician, for the most potent weapons known to mankind are satire and ridicule. It enables him to maintain his perspective and see himself for what he really is.

5. **An organized personality** – He should be able to accept and work with irrationalities for the purpose of change. He should recognize that each person or community has a hierarchy of values. He must become sensitive to every thing that is happening around him. He is always learning and every incident teaches him something. He must also accept without fear or worry that the odds are always against him and be prepared for that.
6. **Free and Open Mind** – He must have a flexible personality, not a rigid structure that breaks down when something unexpected happens. The organizer while working with the community does not have any hidden agenda or pre conceived ideas.
7. **Discerning and Critical Eye** – The organizer should be able to look at the situation and differentiate it critically. Any situation has to be viewed through the eyes of the people carefully and find out its magnitude, symptoms and causes.
8. **Receptive Ear** – The organizer has to be a good and an attentive listener, listening to the people and to their problem. The organizer while working with the community has to be person having patient listening and does not be person commanding over the people.

The difference between a leader and an organizer is – the leader goes on to build power to fulfil his desires to hold and wield the power for purposes both social and personal. He wants power to himself. The organizer finds his goal in creation of power for others to use.

Skills of an Effective Community Organizer

- **Problem Analysis** – One of the major tasks of the community organizer is to assist the people in arriving at a solution to the problem. The organizer is capable of identifying the problem and making the people to identify, analyse, give priorities, select an appropriate priority, mobilize resources, make a plan of action, implement, monitor, evaluate, modify and continue.

- **Resource Mobilization** – Any problem of the community while working out the solution requires resources. The resources may be in terms man power, money material and time. On one hand the organizer is aware of the availability of the resources within the community or outside the community and on the other makes the people to identify the sources of resources and the way to tap such resources.
- **Conflict Resolution** – Problems of the community involves the affected people by the problem and the others who are the causes for the problem. Therefore there could be a conflict between these two groups or between the people and the system. The organizer is equipped with the skill of identifying the conflicting situation and making the people to understand the conflict the work out the ways and means to find solutions to the conflict.
- **Organizing Meeting** – Communication within the community and between the community and the organizer is inevitable. There needs to be transparency in the dealings for which formal and informal meetings have to be organized and information have to be shared. The sharing of information enables sharing of responsibility and decision-making.
- **Writing Reports** – Documentation of the events for future reference and follow up is absolutely essential. Any communication or any written representation and the report of the dealings have to be recorded. This task is either done by the community organizer or delegate the task to some one else for this purpose.
- **Networking** – In a community while working with the people the participation of the people strengthens or increases the power of the people. At times support from like minded people or organization has to elicit so that a pressure is built against the oppressive force and to create pressure and increase the bargaining power for which networking with other people and organization is done by the community organizer.

- **Training** – Capacity building of the people and the personnel of an organization is important while working with the community. In the process of capacity building the community organizer has to be a good trainer. The community organizer has to use his training ability and skills in this regard.

8. Role of a Social Worker in Community Organization Practice

Community organizer having the required characteristics and skills and the knowledge about the process and steps of community organization will be able to apply the same in different settings by appropriate roles. The community organizer has many roles and functions depending upon situation, community and the needs and problems. The roles are as communicator conveys the information, as an enabler, motivator increases the capacity of the community to work towards achieving the goals. The community organizer also acts as a catalyst, consultant and counselor where in he is a source of information and encourages the people to respond to the situation. The community organizer as an innovator suggests new ways and different ways towards the well being of the community. Advocacy is another role where either the organizer represents the community or encourages the community to represent the community whenever needed. The organizer acts neither as a guide nor as a person to dictate or command or demand the members of the community. The organizer has to be a friend, philosopher and guide so that the community is guided and provided with the needed information and enables them to unite their strength and understand their own problem and work out the alternatives in finding solution to the needs and problems.

The different roles of a community organizer are discussed here. These roles are neither exhaustive nor mutually exclusive.

Communicator

The community organizer transfers or transmits information, thought, knowledge etc. to the members of the community. Sharing of information enables the community to be better prepared and empowered with information. The communication between the organizer and the community and within the community is essential. The people have to be prepared and known about the various effects of consequences of the community organization process. The communication takes place by individual contact, group meetings, group discussions, public meetings etc.

At times the community organizer takes an upper hand and considers that the people are illiterate and ignorant and hence the dealings with the people become a master slave relationship. In order to avoid any such undesired relationship the community organizer has transparency and communicates with the people. The communication enables better interaction which leads to a healthy relationship and cooperation for further action and response.

The community organizer in order to disseminate the information to the people can use different techniques like skit, role plays, street plays and audio and vides shows. The organizer can train the people in all these communicative techniques. This will be more effective if he is able to organize the small children and train them in this regard. The children are an effective communicative channel and a fast reaching channel.

The local groups like women's group, youth groups are other channels for communication. By giving the responsibility to such groups to communicate to all other members in the community will also be helpful in reaching out the whole community. There should not be any secrecy or suppression of information which would only create undesired results.

Enabler

The community organizer facilitates the process in the community for a change. He does not carry out any work by himself but he enables the community to do the work. The organizer gives importance to the process than the product. Therefore the people learn the process rather than worried about the results and consequences of the process. By the role of enabler the organizer would create independency among the people by which avoid the dependency syndrome.

The community organizer is present with the people and encourages and gives different directions so that the people are able to decide what they would like to do and how they would like to do. The community organizer only initiates the process and people have to follow and at the time of difficulties they refer back to the community organizer. There fore the role of the community organizer is to make the people to understand the process and to stand on their own.

Animator

In any process of community organization the organizer encourages, provides direction and guide lines to proceed in carrying out the different activities. The people because of their culture always depend on others and do not want to decide anything on their own. In such situation the organizer as an animator makes the people to come forward and take active participation. Any further corrections or modifications in the works of the community are being done by the animator. The animator plays a vital role in eliciting the active participation of the people from planning till evaluation especially ensuring life in all the dealings of the issues and problems.

The people in general do not want to take any risk and at tines they do not even want to do anything for common good. One of the reasons could be that the people have the attitude of culture of poverty or culture of silence. This could be changed by the community organizer by pricking or tickling the conscience of the people through raising questions. This would further enable them increase their level of consciousness.

Guide

The community organizer instead of doing anything on his own guides the members of the community in the process of community organization. The community organizer is not a person to shoulder the responsibility or solving problems of the people. Instead he has to make the people to respond for which the organizer provides the various avenues and shows different roots while dealing with the community problems. As a guide the organizer provides the needed information. He has to be a person with lots of information and ideas. For example in a community there are many educated unemployed youth and their presence in the community is considered to be more of nuisance than as a human resource. In such a situation the community organizer should be able to provide information about the various employment opportunities, and different ways to become self employed, the terms and conditions for availing credit from the credit institutions etc. have to be told to the youth. Once the community organizer is able to provide information which is useful to the people the youth from the neighbouring youth may also approach in getting some guidance from the community organizer. This would surely fetch credit to the community organizer as well as gains the good will of the people.

Counselor

The community organizer understands the community and enables the community to understand itself. At the time of difficulty the individuals or the groups are given the required counseling to proceed in the correct direction. One of the very basic dimensions of counseling is to be a patient listener. Usually every one likes others to listen to them and hesitate to listen to others. Moreover as a counselor he has to step into the shoes of others, understand and respond. People when they are in need there should be some one to listen to them. When people approach there should be some one to attend to. In all such situations the community organizer can easily step in as a counselor in helping the people.

Collaborator

The community organizer joins hands in performing his task with his colleagues with other like minded people and organizations. The organizer has to have interpersonal relationship and public relation skills. Nowadays organizations approach a problem not with their personal capacity they also depend on the neighbouring organization. Similarly other organizations may also look for the cooperation and collaboration of different organization. There are also organization working towards a similar problem where in a collaborative effort will strengthen both the organization. Therefore the role of collaborator is very much needed for net working of similar and like minded organizations and efforts for a common cause.

Consultant

The community organizer enjoys the confidence of the people and advises them in matters of vital interest. The community organizer becomes a person with lots of knowledge and information which is being shared with the people. As a consultant the community organizer makes himself available to the people who are in need because the community organizer has lots of information and expertise which could be availed by those who are in need of it. The community organizer instead of working in the filed in one area will be able to contribute his expertise with many individuals and groups by performing the role of a consultant.

Innovator

The community organizer innovates, performs, and improves the techniques, content in the process of community organization. This gives a lead to the people of the community and enables them to try out new ways and means to find solutions to the needs and problems. The community organization should not be merely for solving problem alone.

On the other hand it has to be in the areas of capacity building of the individuals and community where the organizer can be an innovator by introducing new things to improve the capacity of the people. Community organizer is not a person to maintain the system that exists but he should be a person to introduced new ways and means to climb up the development ladder.

Model

The community organizer commands perfection as a community organizer and serves as a source of inspiration. The role of the organizer is to become an example while working with the people. This should further become as a model which could be applied in other areas with similar problems. By proper planning in approaching a problem and execution of the plan and documenting the whole process will be of greater help to others. The problem solving process becomes a model to others.

Motivator

The community organizer stimulates and sustains active interest among the people for reaching a solution to the needs and problems. The community organizer encourages the community to take up a minor task and complete it successfully which would enable the people to take up difficult task. In such a process the people at times may not take up any initiative or content to live with the existing situation. Therefore, the organizer motivates the people by making them to observe, analyse, understand and respond to the situation. When people are discouraged because they were not able to achieve what they wanted or there is resistance and opposition in such situations the organizer plays the role of a motivator.

Catalyst

In the process of community organization the community organizer retains his identity at the same time enables the people to be empowered. The people gain accessibility and control over resources and acquire skills in decision making.

The community organizer accelerates the actions and reactions so that people are able to achieve the desired results. As a catalyst the organizer is able to increase the response level of the people. The catalyst role further enables the people to become independent and become expert in responding to their own needs.

Advocate

The role of the advocate is to be a representative or persuade the members of the community and prepare them to be a representative as well as represent the issues to the concerned body to bring a solution to the unmet needs. The advocacy role is an important role to the present context. The needs and problems of the people have to be represented and the required support and networking is essential to increase the pressure on the oppressive forces. In the role of advocate the community organizer champions the rights of others. The community organizer speaks on behalf of the community when community is unable to do so, or when community speaks and no one listens. The advocate represents the interests of the community to gain access or services or improve the quality of services which may be hampered by other forces. An advocate argues, debates, bargains, negotiates, and confronts the environment on behalf of the community.

Facilitator

The community organizer helps the community to articulate their needs, clarify and identify their problems, explore resolution strategies, select and apply intervention strategies, and develop their capacities to deal with their own problems more effectively. A facilitator provides support, encouragement, and suggestions to the community so that they may proceed more easily and successfully in completing tasks or problem solving. A facilitator assists the community to find coping strategies, strengths and resources to produce changes necessary for accomplishing goals and objectives. A facilitator helps client systems alter their environment.

Mediator

The community organizer intervenes in disputes between parties to help them find compromises, reconcile differences, or reach mutually satisfying agreements. The mediator takes a neutral stance between the involved parties. A mediator is involved in resolving disputes between members of the between the community and other persons or the broader environment.

Educator

The community organizer as educator conveys information to the community and the broader environment. Organizer provides information necessary for coping with problem situations, assists the community in practising new behaviours or skills, and teaches through modeling. The community organizer provides information necessary for decision making.

Community organization is a macro method in social work. The community organizer with the required qualities and skills will be able to work with the people. While working with the people of different background or from different geographical set up the different roles can be applied. All the roles need not be or cannot be applied in all the settings to all the problems. Moreover there is no one role which is superior or inferior and while dealing with any problem the organizer has to use more than one role. Therefore, depending upon the situation and the needs and problems of the community appropriate role has to be applied.

Levels of Consciousness

It is the understanding of the people about the socio economic status of the people. There are three levels of consciousness namely magic, naïve and critical level.

Magic Level of Consciousness

It is the basic belief in fatalism and justify the status of the person as due to the fate or God's creation.

Naïve Level of Consciousness

People believe that it is due to lack of facilities because of which they are being exploited.

Critical Level of Consciousness

The people understand that due to dependency, inequality and exploitation their status remain as poor.

Empowerment

It is the access and control over self, ideology, resources and decision making.

To work with the community the organizer has to be equipped with lots of skills to deal with the problem on one hand to work with the members of the community. The skill revolves around bridging the gap between the needs and resources. Therefore the community organizer has to equip with the skills of problem solving, resource mobilizing, planning and implementation and evaluation. At the each level the orgazniser has to elicit the participation and cooperation of the people.

Community organization basically involves in preparing the people to identify their own problem, analyse the problem for its magnitude, symptoms and causes. From the problems identified one of the problems is selected based on its severity and urgency. The different ways and means are generated and most appropriate alternative is selected. The needed resources are identified and mobilized. An action is planned to achieve the objectives. This plan is implemented, monitored and evaluated. Based on the evaluation modifications are made if necessary for further action and continued. If the desired plan has been completed the next problem from the priority list is selected for action.

Models and Approaches of Community Organization

Before we proceed to understand the different methods and models of community organization it is wise to understand the terminology. What is a model?

Model

It is a medium through which a person looks at the complex realities. Model is a simplistic version of a complex situation. Models serve as a reference for the work and give us a clear understanding of what would happen. They describe strategies for accomplishing a vision, the appropriate steps to be taken to get there. Some models grow out of the specific ideologies of change and some in response to concrete situations.

Model of Community Organization by Rothman

Since 100 years people in various situations, countries have been trying to address the issues of social welfare. The study of the history helps us to know the drastic changes that took place. A major shift from the charity approach to the professional delivery of services.

Jack Rothman has introduced three basic models of community organization. They are:

Models and Approaches of Community Organization | 59

1. Locality development
2. Social planning
3. Social Action

Model A – Locality Development

Locality development model is a method of working with community groups. It was earlier used by the settlement houses. Here the important focus is about the process of community building. Leadership development and the education of the participants are the essential elements in the process.

According to Murray Ross the "process of self-help and communal action is valuable in its own right". The model of locality development is based on this particular thought process. It originated from the traditional community organization practice. The main focus of this model is whole community or a part of it. The basic belief is that communities have some common needs and interests and once the people realize this need and work together democratically they can take appropriate steps to improve the quality of life.

Here the role of the community organizer is to enhance the involvement of the people in the community and help the community to plan and help them find a solution to the problem. It is similar to work of community development, which is done in the underdevelopment world.

It refers to the community organization practice when a worker or an agency attempts to develop various schemes and programmes to meet the needs of the target population in a defined area. It also includes coordination of various agencies providing a variety of services in the area.

Model B – Social Planning

It refers to the type of community work where a worker or agency undertakes an exercise of evaluating welfare needs and existing services in the area and suggests a possible blue print for a more efficient delivery of services, it is termed as 'social planning'. It is concerned with social problems for example, housing, education, health, childcare and so on. Its aim is to affect a large population. The community planner works in greater capacity with the government and is often identified with power structure of the community but interested in the needs and attitudes of the community.

Model C – Social Action

According to Friedlander, W.A. (1963) "Social Action is an individual, group or community effort within the framework of the social work philosophy and practice that aims to achieve social progress, to modify social policies and to improve social legislation and health and welfare services". Another model of community organization suggested by Rothman is that of social action. According to him social action is a strategy used by groups or sub-communities or even national organizations that feel that they have inadequate power and resources to meet their needs. So they confront with the power structure using conflict as a method to solve their issues related to inequalities and deprivation.

In this type of community organizations the community organizer uses all means to pressure the power structure to give in to demands. The role of organizers may differ depending the issues they get involved in. The role may be of advocate, activist, agitator, broker or negotiator. It is a process. This organizing process goes through different stage. So the role of the organizer will also change as per the roles of the organisor at each stage.

This model was commonly used during the 1960s. This has been used as a means to redress the social problems of the nation, redistribute the resources and power to the poor and powerless. Social action as model has an important role in community organization.

Models of Rothman

It is important to have a theoretical framework to work in the community. This theoretical framework facilitates the

Models and Approaches of Community Organization

worker to adopt strategies and helps him choose the type of focus he/she wants to maintain in the professional practice. Rothman has given three models of practice, which are as follows:

- Neighbourhood development model.
- System Change model.
- Structural change model.

Neighbourhood Development Model

Neighbourhood Model is the oldest model of community organization. This model has been practised in India and in some of the underdeveloped countries. It has been used in the developmental activities. In general it is believed that people living in a neighbourhood have the capacity to meet the problems they come across in their day-to-day life through their own efforts and resources. The main aspect here is that the community realizes its needs and takes appropriate steps to meet the needs of the community, which will bring greater satisfaction to all its members both individually and collectively. The role of the worker in this model is to induce a process that will sensitize the community and make the community realize its needs. Based on the value of self-sustenance the worker energizes the community and makes the community self-reliant, and not merely depending on the help form out side. So rather than providing services in the community, the communities are energized to meet its own needs. This model encourages the people to think for themselves rather than doing things for them.

Some of the steps in this model are:
- Identifying the geographical area for your intervention.
- Making your way to the community.
- Understand the community and identify the felt needs.
- Making an appropriate programme.

- Planning for resource mobilization.
- Developing a strong net-work in the community.
- Planning for withdrawal from the community.

System Change Model

As the name suggests, the system change model aims at developing strategies to either restructure or modify the system. Thus it is termed as "System Change approach" to community work. Although we find glimpses of this model gaining more acceptance, this has not become very popular. We know the various mechanisms that cater to the needs of the society. Such as education, health services, housing, women empowerment, and employment. All these services are rooted through various systems and all these systems do have sub-systems. The fundamental aspect in this model is that the due to various reasons the systems become dysfunctional. For example the system of education as we have it today, reveals that the cities have better educational faculties as compared to the rural areas. This system (education policy) of education has generated disparities in the society. i.e. access to education, lack of basic facilities, trained staff, etc. The system instead of becoming a tool of empowering mechanism brings disparities between people of different socio-economic condition. So the system has failed to achieve its objectives. Thus the worker on observing this disfunction in the community finds it important to develop strategies to restructure or modify the system.

Some of the tasks in this model are:
- Understanding the deficiencies in the system.
- Communicating the findings with the community.
- Making strategies to influence the decision making bodies.
- Mobilizing peoples participation and seeking out-side support to translate the plan in to concrete action.
- Making alliances and partnerships with other NGOs and comminutes to demand a change.

Structural Change Model

One of the most difficult and rarely practised models of community work is structural change model. The society consists of small communities and it is nothing but "a web of relationships". These relationships of the people are formally structured by the respective countries' state policies, law and constitutions and informally by its customs, traditions etc. that determines the social rights of the individuals. The social structure in some of the societies is controlled by the state.

Understanding the macro-structure of social relationship and its impact on the micro-realities, the worker tries to mobilize the public opinion to radically change the macro-structure. Thus the structural change model aims to bring a new social order, an alternative form of society which will transform the existing conditions at the micro-level. This can happen only if an alternative form of political ideology is adopted. This form of community work may originate from a community itself but it has a wider coverage coverage i.e. the entire society or nation. Sometimes this takes the shape of social action, which is an another method of social work profession. Since the general situation in the developing countries is very peculiar, it is very difficult for the community worker to actually practice this model.

A social worker may initiate this model. But it is very difficult to predict the success. However, he s makes attempt to saw the seeds of social change by adopting a political ideology. It might take decades to actually perceive any transformation in the society nevertheless one can be proud of being the agent of social change.

The special tasks involved these models are:
- Understanding the relation ships between macro- and micro social realities.
- Adopting an alternative political ideology.
- Sharing with the family members/faculty members.

- Helping the communities.
- Helping the communities to identify a course of action.

To prepare the community to sustain its interests, enthusiasm and capacity to met the strains that may arise out of the conflict with the existing power structure.

Approaches to Community Organization

The history has witnessed diversity of efforts in the community organization and the emergence of new initiatives in the field. Most often these of community organizing efforts are centred on identity communities and issue - specific communities. History gives us a list of different kind of community organizing methods. One such community organizing which the twentieth century has witnessed is the growth of neighborhood organizing.

Neighbourhood Organizing

Neighbourhood organizing is one form of community organizing. This nothing but an effort by the community to solve the day-to-day problems and help those in need.

There are three types of approaches to neighbourhood organizing:

1. The social work approach
2. The political activists approach
3. Neighborhood maintenance/community development approach

The Social Work Approach

In this approach, the society is viewed as a social organism and therefore the efforts are oriented towards building a sense of community. The community organizer whose role is of an "enabler or an advocate" helps the community identify a problem in the neighborhood and strives to achieve the needed social resources by gathering the existing the social services and by lobbying with some in power to meet the needs of the neighborhood. This method is more consensual and the neighborhood is seen as a collective client. One example of this approach is the social settlement movement U.S.A. and war on poverty programme of the Johnson administration in the 1960s.

The Political Activists Approach

Saul Alinsky, the Godfather of community organizing is the founder of this approach. He emerged as a community organizer in the 1930s.The basic philosophy of this approach is based on his thinking that "more representative the organization the stronger the organization".

In this approach the community is seen as a political entity and not as a social organism. Here, the neighbourhood is viewed as a potential power base capable of getting power. The role of the community organizer is to help the community understand the problem in terms of power and necessary steps are taken to mobilize the community. The problem of the neighbourhood is always identified as absence of power and in the interest of gaining power for the neighborhood the organizers are faced with conflicts with groups, interests and elities. Since most of the community organizers come from out side the community, it has faced the problems of equality of power relations and leadership in the community.

Unlike the social work approach to community organization this approach has the potential to create stable, democratic and effective organizations of neighborhood residents by seeing its role as "meeting power with power".

Neighborhood Maintenance/Community Development Approach

This approach has emerged out of both the previous approaches namely within the same neighborhood movements. It is seen in the form of civic associations. This association uses peer group pressure to provide services in the community. They use this strategy to pressurize the officials to deliver services to the community but sometimes this approach takes the form of political activists approach as they realize that their goals can be only achieved only through confrontations.

In this approach we see the characteristics of de-emphasis on dissent and confrontation and these organizations view themselves as more proactive and development minded.

10. Basic Steps in Community Organization

The following are the basic steps of community organization practice:

Identifying the Problem

Under this step the following information is gathered:
1. Nature of the problem.
2. Severity of the problem.
3. Implication of the problem.
4. Location (institutional/social).
5. Causation of the problem.
6. Recognition of the need for change.
7. Scope of the problem (who are affected).
8. Efforts made to solve the problem.
9. Effectiveness of the previous efforts.
10. Reasons for success or failure.

Perception of the Problem - Facts and Data
1. Attitude of the community.
2. Perception of the problem.
3. Significant different attitudes.

Structural - Functional Analysis

1. Origin of the problem.
2. Characteristics of community structure that maintains problem.
3. Forces operating favourably and unfavourably.
4. Significant elements of social structure.

Beneficiaries Profile

1. Population segments.
2. Physical surroundings of the community.
3. Factors operating as behaviour determinants.
4. Clients divisional cleavages.
5. Significant relations with other parts of social structure.
6. Level of acceptance of plans.
7. Barriers into the way of acceptance.
8. Significance of the barriers.

Action Plan

1. Thinking of various possible courses of action.
2. Analysis of the course of action in terms of cost, efforts, consequences, effectiveness, acceptability.
3. Selecting the best possible course of action.
4. Analysis of the problem-solving structure and processes.

Determination of Strategy

1. Level of efforts required for success.
2. Nature of activities required.
3. Minimum work required.
4. Action system - Individual conscientization, group conscientization, organization and planning, building and maintaining viable counter system, developing skills, administrative techniques.

Linking People with the Programme

1. *Areas*
   - Level of need analysis.
   - Nature of activities required.
   - Strategy Determination.
   - Planning action.
   - Implementation and Management.
2. *Approaches*
   - Individual approach.
   - Extensive approach.
   - Community education.
   - Need-base approach.
   - Social action.
3. *Steps to be taken*
   - Arousal of consciousness about problem.
   - Popularization of the problem.
   - Creation of motivating force for solving the problem.
   - Suggestion invitation.
   - Rendering proper knowledge.
   - Resource utilization.
   - Promotion for action of practice.
   - Regular contact.
   - Follow up.

Implementation and Evaluation

1. Effectiveness of action.
2. Success of strategy in problem solving.
3. Weakness in action.
4. Designing new strategy and action.

Building Counter System

Aims to develop a power base from which changes in existing system can be achieved.

11. Relevance of Community Organization in Community Development

Community organization and community development are inter-related. To achieve the goals of community development the community organization method is used. According to United Nations, community development deals with total development of a developing country that is economic, physical, and social aspects. For achieving total development community organization is used. In community development the following aspects are considered as important. The same aspects are also considered as important by community organization. They are:

(a) Democratic procedures.

(b) Voluntary cooperation.

(c) Self-help.

(d) Development of leadership.

(e) Educational aspects.

All the above aspects are related with community organization.

Democratic procedures deal with allowing all the community members to participate in decision-making. It is possible to achieve this by community organization. The selected or elected members or representatives are helped to take decisions. Democratic procedures help people to take part in achieving community development goals. Community organization method permits the democratic procedures for people's participation

Voluntary cooperation means the people are suppose to volunteer for their participation. For this they are convinced. They should feel that they should involve in the process of development without hesitation. This is supported by community organization method. People's emotional involvement is necessary according to community organization method. If discontentment is created properly then people will volunteer for participation. Community organization emphasizes the discontentment and people's participation.

Self-help is the basis for community development. Self-help deals with the capacity of mobilizing internal resources. Self-help is the basis for self-sufficiency and sustainable development. In community organization self-help is emphasized. Community organization is relevant to community development because both emphasizes the self-help concepts.

Development of leadership is an important aspect in community development. Leadership deals with influencing people to achieve the goals. Community organization also emphasizes leadership. With the help of leaders the people are motivated to participate in action. Community organization is a relevant method to develop and use leadership. So it is applicable for community development.

Educational aspects in community development means helping people to know, learn, many of the aspects like, democracy, cooperation, unity, skill development, effective functioning etc.

In community organization the above mentioned aspects are considered as important. The process of community organization emphasizes education of the community. Thus both are emphasizing educational aspects of the community. Thus community organization and community development are interrelated and relevant. There are no opposing aspects in between community organization and community development and both emphasize the same aspects. Thus they are relevant. So in all community development programmes community organization method is used as implementing method.

Distinction Between Community Organization and Community Development

There are many similarities between community organization and community development. But for theoretical purpose it is possible to differentiate community organization and community development:

(a) Community organization is a method of social work but community development is a programme for a planned change.

(b) Community organization emphasizes the processes, but community development emphasizes the end or goals.

(c) Community organizers are mostly social workers and social change agents, but community development personnel can be from other professions such as economics, agricultural experts, veterinary experts, and other technical experts.

(d) Community organization is not time bound. It is achieved step by step according to the pace of the people. But community development is time bound and time is specified for achieving the development.

(e) In community organization people's participation is important. But in community development people's development is important.

(f) In community organization government and external agencies, assistance is not important and needed. But in community development external assistance from the government is considered as important.

(g) Community organization is a method of social work and this method is used in many fields, but unlike community organization community development is considered as process, method, programme, and movement for planned change.

(h) Community organization is used in all the fields but community development is used in mostly economic development and for the development of living standards of the people.

(i) In community organization planning is initiated by the people participation. But in community development planning is carried out by an external agency mostly by the government.

(j) In community organization people are organized to solve their problem. But in community development goals have to be achieved and for that people are organized.

(k) Community organization is universal to all communities. But community development programmes differ from people to people and according to the nature of the country.

Even though there are differences, but both are inter-related. The relationship is so close, so that community organization process and principles are accepted fully. Both are like two sides of the same coin. The ideal community development is where community organization method is used without any mistake.

Working with Individuals, Families, and Groups within the Community

Individuals join together and constitute groups and families. Families and groups join together and form communities. While working with communities we have to work with individuals, families, and groups. In actual practice of social work distinction between different practices of social work methods do not have clear boundaries. All are carried out based on the situation. In community organization the organizer has to work with individuals. Individual contact strategy is used to create awareness. Individually people are motivated to accept community goals through education and awareness. Working with individuals takes much time but it is very effective and successful. Working with families and groups cannot be avoided in community organization. Working with many groups is considered as community organization. In the community there are many groups. For achieving the common goals we have to work with different groups. There are many groups in the community involved in different activities. They are dependent on each other for their functioning. The community organizer works with the groups in order to articulate with one other to achieve the goals of the community. Thus the community organizer takes deliberate efforts to influence the unity among individuals, families, and groups. When they unite together they collaborate to achieve the common goals. Groups are considered superior than Individuals in problem solving and action. The groups are better than the average individual but they are not better than the best individual. They may not perform well when compared to one expert. While working with groups there is a possibility of getting variety of opinions and information for community organization. The group members can eliminate the unwanted opinions by group decisions. The individuals can work fast in a group but to involve in work takes some time. Consensus is considered as an ideal way to select among alternatives while working with groups because; the group members commit themselves for the cause or decision. When there are controversial issues among the group members, it is possible to reach a decision by modifying the original decision. Then it is acceptable to all the group members. Thus a community organizer can work with individuals and groups to achieve the community goals. The organizer should know casework and group work skills apart from community organization skills to work with individuals and groups in the community.

Understanding Power in the Context of Community Organization

Concept of Power

Power means an ability to influence, in community organization. That is influencing community members to act up on as directed by the leaders to achieve the community goals. The community power aspects can be studied. This is called as power structure of the community. The power structure of the community varies according to the community.

The Dimensions of Power

According to social workers, power is the ability to influence the beliefs and behaviour of others according to wish or plan. In other words, power is the ability to make things happen. Floyd Hunter explained the nature of power and power structure. Power appears in numerous forms and in a variety of combinations. Power flows from many sources. The money, votes, laws, information, expertise, prestige, group support, contacts, charisma, communication channels, media, social role, access to rewards, position, titles, ideas, verbal skill, ability to gratify important needs, monopoly of essential resources, alliances, energy, conviction, courage, interpersonal skills, moral convictions, etc. are some of the sources of power. The accumulation of power in a specific area is called as a power center. Power is also distributed. It is not confined within the power center. It is present at every level of the society. The powerless people do have power. They have to discover their power. Power may be ascribed by formal delegation or by title. Power may be achieved by many ways. For example, through competence, ability, or by personality etc. power can be achieved. Generally groups of people are at the top of the community. They are called as power centres at the top of the power pyramid. They influence the community through formal and informal connections. They influence through subordinate leaders who do not participate in community decision-making process. The rich people are mostly powerful. In some communities multiplicity of power structure is noticed. Power structure is also flexible in nature. The community organizer has to study the following: How do some people influence the action of others? Who wields the power? How? What are the issues? What are the results? These aspects are to be analyzed by the organizer for effective practice of community organization. This is called as community power structure analysis. It is called as power because some people are capable of action in spite of the resistance of others who are participating in the action. Some people are powerful because they knew each other personally and they interact frequently making them involve in joint efforts in community affairs. People with power, make major community decision where as others are active in implementing such decisions. An organizer who is able to study the power structure well can practice community organization effectively. For example, the village traditional leader is a powerful person. The leader can influence other people to act. Many times this leader is motivated to involve in achieving the goals of the community. The leader is capable of influencing people effectively. When there is opposition from a few men, it can be tackled by the leader because the leader has power.

In the community power is distributed. Each power center tries to expand its influence over the distribution of resources and rewards. The various power centers enter into an alliance. They share power, enter into a contract and discharge obligations. Power does not come to the passive, timid, defeated, persons. Energetic, courageous, persons wield it. The people with power tend to join together based on issues. The basis for alliance are ideological, personality similarities, needs, or to achieve the goals. Power possessed is always used. It can be used for achieving the goals. The power can be intellectual, political, social, and psychological power. To retain power there is a need for self-awareness and self control. The decision-making is the source and out come of the power. Some times there is a possibility of many number of power centers. Each power center may be autonomous. The organizer needs knowledge, and ability to mobilize the power in the community for achieving the goals of the community.

There are techniques for mobilization of power:

(a) Appealing to the persons with power, who are related with achieving the goal.
(b) Relating the power centers directly to the goal.
(c) Developing interdependence among power centers for fulfilling the goals.
(d) Formation of new groups by including members of power centers to achieve the goals.
(e) Encouraging members of power centers to join with other members of power centers to achieve the goal.
(f) By using group work methods, new larger power centers can be strengthened to achieve the goals.

Saul Alinsky and Richard Cloward used the changing of power centres. [1960]. The power centre change is achieved by institutional changes. Saul Alinsky gave importance for grass-root approach. In grass-root approach lower level people should get deciding power. Power and authority are connected. Authority is the legitimatization of power. These details are used in community organization to achieve people's participation and successful achievement of the goal.

The Relevance of Power in Community Organization

Development is influenced by power structures of the community. People who are influential can mobilize a major segment of the community. For example; in fund raising drive some people can move behind other people and institutions. There are two models of community power structure. The stratification model and the pluralist mode are the two models of power structures. Stratification model suggests that social class principally determines the distribution of community power. According to this model the power structure in community is composed of stable upper class elite whose interest and out look on community affairs are relatively homogeneous. According to pluralist model, it rejects the idea that a small homogeneous group dominates community decision-making.

But there are numerous small special interest groups that cut across class lines, which are represented in the community decision-making. These are interest groups with overlapping memberships, widely differing power bases, have influences on decisions. Community decisions are the result of the interactions of these different interest groups. This theoretical orientation can help the community organizer in his action. The organizer has to identify the members of the power structure for community organization.

Floyd Hunter an executive director of a community welfare council wrote classic volumes on community power structure. His method of locating community elites is known as the reputation approach. The basic procedure is to ask a group of informants who are knowledgeable about the community to list the people they believe to be most influential in the community affairs. There may be variations on this procedure with regard to how informants are selected, and how questions are put in. By tallying those people most frequently named as influential leaders we can identify the core of the community power structure.

Position approach is another method of locating the members of the power structure based on the assumption of stratification model. This approach assumes that people holding the highest office in the community are at the top of the power structure. By scanning the executive lists of the important social political and economic organizations in the community, one can quickly compile a list of members of the power structure. This approach requires fewer efforts than the reputation approach. Community power is directly related with community organization. Participation of people is related with power.

In community organization community power holders are involved to induce people's participation in order to achieve the organizations objectives. Some times if the existing power centers are not for community organizational objectives, then a new center of power is created to get people's commitment and mass participation. The organizer needs to study power structure and community organization process is carried out successfully through leaders. For example, people are organized to implement family planning. For this the leader is motivated for people's participation. In some villages the leader opposes family planning.

In this situation the community organizer has to identify a new powerful leader to implement family planning. Other wise it is not possible to implement family planning in the village.

Barriers of Empowerment

Generally poor people have the feeling of powerlessness. These people can be helped to feel powerful to decide their own affairs using community organization. When they learn to solve their problems they feel powerful. We can develop confidence and capacity building so that they feel that they can solve their problems by themselves. In community organization, the people carry out decision-making. This provides them with a sense of empowerment. Empowerment deals with providing disadvantaged groups with a powerful instrument for articulating their demands and preferences by awareness, decision-making capacity and to achieve their goal with freedom.

Community organization results in empowerment of the people. But there are some hindrances like fatalism, illiteracy, superstitions, and caste divisions etc. Some times the vested interested groups may be a hindrance or barriers for empowerment. The community dependence, long time effect of poverty, and wrong beliefs etc., act as barriers to empowerment. When people are organized, they get the power. There are leaders in the community, they are united, they can work together, and they can co ordinate with each other. This makes them feel powerful. Thus community organization results in empowerment of people. The empowerment helps the community to stand against exploitation, ability to solve problems, and to achieve the desired goals. Many of the economic problems can be easily solved by community organization and empowerment of community.

13 Current Issues in Community Organization

The social life of the people is affected by the kind of community in which they live. With the advancement of science our life has become complex. Self-sufficiency of village communities has broken down. Social institutions like family, joint family, caste system, village panchayat; private property, education etc. have undergone changes. And are not able to meet the changing demands of the individual and community.

The communities of toady are facing lots of challenges. The ancient social relations, emotional bonds and sentimental ties are no more significant and visible. The community consciousness is rapidly lowering down. Dirty politics has housed into the peaceful life of the community people and they are divided into different political groups and sub-groups. The joint family system is fast disintegrating and strains on human mind are increasing. Communal disharmony, gender inequality, factionalism, protection of rights of marginalized groups, feelings of deprivations among different classes like cultivators, industrial workers, daily wage earners, alteration of property relations in favour of the less privileged and impact of macro policies at micro levels are the some current issues which require immediate intervention while working with communities, institutions and organizations. This unit gives you a broad understanding of issues, which are affecting the dynamics of the healthy life styles and functioning of the communities and organizations. Let us now understand the meaning of gender, difference between gender and sex, gender system and its elements and impact of gender system on women inequalities.

Gender Sensitive Community Organization Practice

The *Oxford Dictionary* meaning of gender is sexual classification, i.e. male and female. But gender is not biological attribute. It is created by the society as a set of system. There is a need of a 'system of equal existence' of 'Men' and 'Women'. Unfortunately, our present system is involved in developing its own set of rules, which is basically responsible for discrimination and injustice of women and girl child in our society.

Difference Between Gender and Sex

Gender	Sex
Socially defined	Biologically defined
Socio-cultural difference	Natural difference
Made by the society	Naturally made.
Variable	Constant

Gender gives different values to men and women. The biological sex differences are accepted as correct indicator for differential male-female access and their participation in the society. Our society is organized around some given parameters and aims, the functionality of which is ensured by a set of systems and institutions. For instance, marriage and family life are ingrained aspects of the Indian Society. Girls and boys get married and start their own families living within the prescribed norms that determine choice of marriage partner, their roles, code of conduct (fidelity, chastity, girl's subservience to her husband and in-laws), life-style and practices (such as *purda*, male inheritance, dowry etc.) One of the most pervasive and widespread codes of organization that affects all aspects of social functioning is the gender system. It is patriarchy that provides the life force to the unfavourable conditions that woman face. Let us try and list out some of the more common features of gender system.

Male-Female Differentiation

The practices of male-female differentiation form the core of a gender-based system. Biological sex differences, which are real, are extended to be the criteria for social placement.

Allocation of Roles

In any organization or society roles are attributed for specific function. In a patriarchy, roles are allocated not only in accordance with the biological functions (procreation), but are misappropriated according to values prescribed to male and females. Within patriarchy 'dominating and controlling social functions are prescribed for males whereas 'supportive functions are the purview of the females. Thus, by birth, the males are 'inheritors of resources', performing the functions of earners and by birth the females are 'family caretakers' performing the functions of 'child nurturing and running the householder'.

Gender-based Hierarchical Placement

Along with role allocation certain norms and values, as well as practices and beliefs, further promote the 'male-female superior-inferior or hierarchy', whereby males have access to land holdings inheritance, skills, productive employment and the associated high status, women, on the other hand are denied even life (female infanticide/foeticide), receive poor nutrition and medical care, inferior education and suffer atrocities such as eve teasing, rape, wife-beating etc.

Elements of the Gender System

The female biological functions of reproduction are extended to rearing of children and catering to household work. On the other hand the role of the male is to earn for the family. Accordingly, both sexes are socialized to these predetermined but separate roles. Even in society where both men and women are called upon to earn, the primary roles associated with social values have remained unchanged. Thus even if women earn an income, their responsibility towards household chores remains undiminished.

Caste and class both are status groups. A status group is an association of individuals who enjoy a distinctive style of life and a certain consciousness of kind. However, castes are perceived as hereditary groups with a fixed ritual status while classes are defined in terms of the relations of production. The members of a class have a similar socio-economic status in relation to other classes in the society, while the members of a caste have either a high or a low ritual status in relation to other castes.

Caste as a Unit and as a System

Caste is considered viewed both as a unit and as a system. It is also understood as a structural phenomenon as well as a cultural phenomenon. As a unit, caste can be defined as a 'closed rank status group', that is a group in which the status of the members, their occupation, the field of mate selection and interaction with others is fixed. As a system, it refers to interrelated status and patterned interaction among castes in terms of collectivity of restrictions, namely, restriction on change of membership, occupation, marriage and communal relations. In viewing caste as a system, there is pre-supposition that no caste can exist in isolation and that each caste is closely involved with other castes in the network of economic, political, and ritual relationships. The 'closed-rank group' feature of caste also explains its structure. As a cultural phenomenon, caste may be viewed as a "set of values, beliefs and practices".

A social class is "one of two or more broad groups of individual who are ranked by the members of the community in socially superior and inferior positions". (Ginsberg, Morris: 1961). Thus, in a social class there is:

- *A feeling of equality* in relation to members of one's own class.
- *A consciousness* that one's mode of behaviour will harmony with the behaviour of similar standards of life.
- Individuals belonging to the same social class are expected *to maintain similar standards of life.*
- Choose their occupations within a limited range.
- There is *realization of similarity of attitude and behaviour* with the members of one class.
- There is a *feeling of inferiority* in relation to those who stand above in the social scale.

There is a feeling of superiority to those below in social hierarchy.

Axis of Inequality of Caste and Class

If we look at our society, we find that people are divided in categories (in castes and classes) on the basis on birth, religion, race, language and speech, education, occupation and wealth etc. and society is heterogeneous in nature. Individuals are placed higher or lower in a status scale based on these characteristics. Thus social barriers are erected in the way of lower category (caste and class) people's overall development. This has given birth to several inequalities:

Caste

- lestricts mobility of working class especially of marginalized;
- leads to untouchability, slavery and is responsible for many other social evils and vices like child marriage, dowry system, purda system and casteism;
- responsible for low status of women;
- is bed-rock of religious discrimination and fundamentalism.

Class

- The dream to alter property-relations in favour of less privileged has yet to see ray of the day.

Further the persisting inter and intra-caste, class and community inequalities as well as wide spread unrest are also result of prevailing contradictions in our social system. Such as:

- We continue to follow the traditional values whereas our roles have become modern.
- We profess that India is committed to bring equality but in reality it is mired in an age-old system of caste and class.
- We claim ourselves as rationalist but we bear with injustice and unfairness with fatalistic resignation.
- We speak in favour of individualism but we reinforce collectivism.

In spite of formulation of so many laws and modification of old laws, the common people have not been benefitted from these because they are either not being implemented or are full of loopholes which have benefited only to legal profession.

Settings of Community Organization Practice in Social Work

There are different areas where community organization has scope. The community organizer can practise community organization in such settings. The settings can be identified based on certain characteristics such as location and the nature of administration.

- Geographical location rural, urban, tribal.
- Sector institutional, non-institutional or organized, unorganized.
- Model locality development.
- Social planning.

Social Action

The target group with whom the community organizer is going to work with has to be identified and understood. The needs and problems of the community in different settings need not be the same and moreover the characteristics of the people in different settings are likely to vary and hence accordingly the methods and techniques of community organization and the roles of community organizer have to be used.

The organizer can use different methods to identify, assess the need, analyse and understand the situation. There are two levels of understanding the first level understanding of the community by the organizer and the second level is making the community to understand their own situation. Different methods and techniques can be used to understand and make the community to understand. Participatory Rural Appraisal (PRA) and Appreciative Inquiry can be more useful in this regard. Since these are not the scope of this unit it is not discussed here.

What ever may be the settings there is a community or a group of people with needs and problems. In other words there is discontentment which has to be focused and chanalised in such a way that the people come together, think together, plan together, implement and evaluate their actions. In all the stages the community is fully involved and their capacity is increased in terms of access and control over resources and decision making. Therefore in community organization the community organizer has to play different roles in making the people to be on their own without any dependency syndrome.

Though the types of settings have limited classification it can be said that where ever there are people or the like minded people or the affected people come together and can form a community in acquiring their due share from the society.

In different settings depending on the needs and problems and the situation of the community the roles and strategies have to be changed. Moreover all the roles need not be applied in all the settings. In order to adopt different roles the community organizer has to be very clear about the process or the steps involved in the practice of community organization methods and skills and accordingly the roles can be selected and applied.

Rural area is differentiated with urban based on the population size, density of population and occupation of the people. In any area the population is more than 5000, the density is more than 300 per square kilometre and more than 75 per cent of the people are engaged in agricultural activities such areas are called rural area. Along with these characteristics if the geographical location in general is in the hills it is called the tribal area. In the case of urban the population is more than 5000, density is more than 300 per square kilometer and more than 75 per cent are involved in non agricultural activities.

Among the people inter personal relationship and receptiveness is high and positive in rural and tribal areas where as in urban area the primary relationship within the community is rather low. Organizing rural and tribal people is less difficult compared to urban people.

In the institutional and non institutional settings the people are organized and not organized respectively. In an institution due to the organizational structure there is possibility to bring the people together for any common purposed whereas in the case of non institutional there is not a structured pattern and hence it may be difficult to bring them together.

The three models of community organization expect different sets of roles. In locality development model the people come together to discuss and decide about the improvement of an area, or locality, emphasizing the broader participation at the local level in goal determination and action.

In the social planning model the people come together and gather pertinent facts about the problems, then decide on a rational and feasible course of action. It is a technical process of solving social problems. Arranging and delivering goods and services to people whom need them. External help is more. Interested group members participate. Broader participation is less.

Social action model brings the people to destroy the oppressors. Basic changes in major situations are brought about by organizing the segment of the population so that they make demands on the larger community for increased resources or treatment more in accordance with social justice and democracy and redistribution of power, resources and decision-making.

The community organizer has to see, observe and understand all the settings and the models before responding or making the people to respond to the situation.

This could be otherwise called as assessment of needs and problems of the community. Community organizer has to know about the needs and problems at the same time he has to enable the people to make an assessment of the needs and problems. In order to do this process the community has to come forward to realize and express for further action or response individually or collectively. In this process the people get empowered by way of acquiring the skills of analysis and raising the levels of consciousness.

List the Problems

All the identified needs and problems of the community are listed by the community with the help of the community organizer. This is a process which makes the people to understand their own situation. Realization of the needs and problems will bring awareness about their own situation. The involvement of the community in identifying the various needs and problems will increase the participation of the people. The problems in different settings are likely to differ and hence accordingly the identified problems are listed.

Give Priorities

All the needs and problems cannot be considered together for further action. Therefore, all the needs and problems are analysed for its severity, magnitude, symptoms and causes based on which they are ordered and priority is given to all the needs and problems. The community after having identified the needs and problems analysis them and give priority by which they have to be taken up for further actions.

Select a Problem

From the priority list most urgent problem which needs to be taken up immediately is selected. All the problems cannot be approached simultaneously therefore there is need for selecting any one problem and initiate further action. Based on the order of priority the first in the list is taken up for working out solutions.

Redefine the Problem

The selected problem is redefined for better understanding by the community. For better planning the problem has to be analysed and defined before taking any further step in addressing the problem. Many a times one may look at a phenomenon as a problem by its appearance or at the peripheral level instead it has to be further analysed is it a real problem. Does it affect the normal functioning of the community? How many people are being affected? How are they affected? If nothing is does towards this how it will disturb the community? These are all some of the questions by which we can easily analyse and understand to redefine the problem.

Formulate Achievable Objective

The redefined problem is converted into achievable objectives which will be considered for further action. At times the objectives have to be split into many parts so that they could be converted in to programmes and activities towards fulfilling the needs and problem. Let us assume that illiteracy is a problem in a community. It is further analysed that majority of the people of the locality have not gone to school at their childhood days. One of the reasons for that was that there was no school in their locality. At present a school has been constructed and teachers are appointed. Now non availability of the school is not the reason for illiteracy. It is further analysed and found that the children are not sent to the school. Though there were many children at the school going age the parents do not send them to the school because the teachers are not regular on one hand and on the other when the teachers are present they do not teach the children. In this situation the general problem externally appears to be illiteracy but its root cause is the defective function of the school.

Work out the Alternatives

Based on the objectives the different ways and means are found out by the community through brain storming. One should not be content with a problem with one solution because it will limit the practice of community organization. In order to solve the selected problem the community has to generate maximum number of alternatives to address the problem. Let us take the problem of illiteracy as stated in the previous stage. How do we solve the problem? The problem is directly related to the defective functioning of the school. What are the different ways to solve this? The concerned teachers can be met and advised. The defective functioning can be brought to the notice of the higher authorities. The higher authorities can be met by the representatives with a written representation. Motivate more children to join the school. Withdraw all the children from the school. Close the school. Organize a protest march. Organize a hunger strike. There could be many such alternatives could be generated in tackling any problem.

Select an Appropriate Alternative

Among the proposed alternatives one of the best alternatives is selected for tackling the selected problem. To solve a problem there could be many ways but there may be one best and suitable way or method by which the problem could be easily solved. Such options should be selected. While selecting an alternative one has to start with softer approach and in a sequence. If the lower level approach fails apply the next one and even that one fails then select the next one and nothing works out finally we may resort to social action methods and may be at times we may have to resort to strong measures.

Work Out a Plan of Action

In order to materialize the selected alternative an action plan is proposed in which the responsibilities are assigned and tentative organization is structured. The time frame, resources needed and personnel involved are decided at this stage. Supposing to solve the illiteracy problem of a community it is decided to meet the authorities to present a petition. This has to be discussed at length to decide about the date, time, who, how many, where etc. At the time of meeting the authorities who is to speak? What to speak? How to speak? All these things have to be decided and role played so that it is done in a perfect manner and brings the desired results.

Mobilization of Resources

To implement the plan of action the required resources is assessed, identified and mobilized. The resources may be in terms of time, money, man power and material. An estimate is made and the sources are identified for mobilizing the resources. Many a times man power resources alone may help to arrive at a solution. Therefore, the community has to have a thorough understanding by which people by themselves may come forward to include themselves for further action. Apart from this any other resources have to be mobilized internally and if it is not possible then we have to think about it from external sources.

Implement the Plan of Action

After having made a plan of action along with the resources the plan is implemented. The implementation takes care of the time and resources towards fulfilling the fixed goals. While implementing the plan of action the involvement of the people and their active participation by accepting the responsibilities has to be ensured. The people have to be prepared and guided to become a partner in the problem solving approach.

Evaluate the Action

The implemented plan is evaluated to find out the success and deviancy of the action from the objectives. Any deviancy or any undesired results are identified and the reasons for the deviancy are discussed. The positive and desired results are to be appreciated. The evaluation can be made as one of the components of working with the community. It could be organized either at periodical level or at the end of the activity either within the organization by the organization personnel or by an outsider or by an expert. The task is not complete unless the evaluation is completed.

Modification

Based on the evaluation the modification needed is decided and introduced. In order to bring a permanent solution to the selected problem it is being addressed with the modifications. These modifications are proposed in order to settle the problem permanently.

Continuation

The modified action plan is implemented and continued.

Select the Next Problem

Once the selected need is fulfilled the next problem is selected from the priority list.

Community Welfare Planning

Planning is an important aspect of community organization. Planning for health and social welfare is a process through which individuals, groups and the community decide those conditions, programmes and facilities, establish and maintain those which in their opinion secure them from disrupting the group life and make it possible to achieve and maintain a high standard of welfare.

Community welfare planning means seeking public support, disseminate important and neede information, appoint appropriate communities, listening opposing point of view, their analizes and bringing about, compromise in opposite feelings are all included. All method which are used in community organization are also used in community planning. The basic facts and strengths within the community are used for a sound planning for health and social welfare. Community planning is used for geographical area from the smallest local area to the national level planning.

Planning means to formulate beforehand what efforts are recquired to be made in the future. Planning means to clarify the objectives which are planned to be fulfilled for social welfare, to clarify them and to work on them i.e. what method or procedures are to be adopted. What would be level of the quality or experiences involved in performing and using a particular method. How that activity is to be supported. All these are decided before hand.

Planning is a established fact. A group and a mutually dependentant community depends finally on planning process to provide a wholesome life to its members. Planning means to bring about orderly thinking in community life because planning thinking has a conscious objective direction so that those goals and objectives on which there is common agreement are fulfilled through the creation of reasonable means. In planning priorities are always decided essentially and basic decision are required to be taken. Planning is the basic and major method of solving those human problem faced by individuals groups or the community.

Planning is a point of view, and attitude and assumption which tells us as to what is; possible and we can make an assessment of our destiny, make predictions and can guide and control our action for achieving our goals. When we accept the concept of community planning, we explain the philosophy behind our functioning or we express our complete views about individuals, and their capability of controlling their own future.

A professional worker and special skills are needed in planning. The use of this skills clarifies five dimensions of planning.

Professional skill is essential for the establishment of a continues process by means of which problem of community are recognised.

1. Professional skill is essential for the establishment of a process of collection of data or facts so that all information about the problem is easily disseminated.
2. The use of professional skill is essential for the creation of a functional method for the formulation of a plan or project.
3. In the whole process of community organization, formulation of a plan is only a dot. What happens before and after the formulation of a plan is more important.
4. Professional skill is neede in deciding procedures in trhe implementation of the plan.

Planning is not done in a vaccum. Goals are needed for it. Some achievements should be the result of a plan. Objectives are in fact a map which shows us where we have to go and which means we can adopt. We must have a full knowledge of the community in which we go for the practice of community organization. For major areas which help us in deciding the objectives are functions of social work, the role of the agency or institution in the community, special needs of the group and special needs of the individuals.

In order to create psychological readiness and planning, professional help is provided by the community organiser. It needs to be understood that planning is a positive process, not a negative one. There should be no fear of planning that there is some sort of super control somewhere in the process or its implementation. Partial planning is not desirable.

Principles of Planning

Among the principles of planning, those important principles which have equal importants in the practice of Community organization have been mentioned by Trecker as follows:

1. In order to be effective planning should originate from the interest and needs of those individuals who form an agency.
2. In order to be effective, those persons who are to be effected by planning should be participants in the formulation of the plan.
3. To be more effective, planning should have an adovocate factual base.
4. More effective plans originate from that process in which there is a mixture of methods of face to face contact and the method of more formal committee work.
5. Because of differences in the circumstances, there should be individualization and specialization in the planning process, ie., plans should be formulated according to local conditions.
6. A professional leader is needed in planning.
7. In addition to the efforts of volunteers, nonprofessional individuals and community leaders, the efforts of professional workers are also needed in planning.
8. The maintenance of documents and complete records is needed in planning inorder to secure the community of the results of the discussions and directions.
9. The ongoing plans and resources should continue to be used and work shouldnot be started afresh for the solution of each and every new problem.
10. Planning depends on prior thinking before action starts.

The importance of peoples participation in planning should not be considered less. The members of the community should participate fully in all stages of the process of planning and its implementation.

Three Contrary Views

There are three main strands in these criticisms. The first is concerned with the emphasis placed on cooperation in our conception of community organization. There would be some who would suggest that there is little evidence to indicate that cooperative work brings the kind of results we imply in all, or even a majority of, situations. Further, it could be argued that the emphasis on cooperation as a primary good, which seems implicit in our thesis is hardly justifiable in light of competing goods. Therefore some would suggest that our interpretation of community organization overvalues and overstressed cooperation.

A second critical view is that community organization interferes with the way people choose, desire, or want to live, and that in many situations it tends to manipulate ideas and people to secure the ends of a professional elite.

A third strand of criticism implies that however justifiable the community organization process may be in philosophical terms, it is not practical in a society in which "cultural lag" becomes more pronounced every day. Change in our way of living must come quickly, it can be imposed, and people will adjust to the new objective situation.

Value Assumptions

A simple response to these counterviews would be that community organization as it is defined here, doesn't make cooperation an ultimate good, doesn't deny the value of individual effort, doesn't insist that all goals can be achieved only in cooperative work. Similarly it could be said that the particular conception of community organization outlined here has no tolerance for manipulation but it is disposed towards "open covenants openly arrived at". Nor does this interpretation of community organization imply denial of the validity and value of other approaches to the solution of the problems of community life (e.g., the need for the planning by social scientists, housing, traffic, zoning, and other types of experts) but asserts that the development of "Community" (both geographic and functional), as interpreted here, is essential if the values implicit in the concept of democracy are to be maintained.

Community organization derives from a unique frame of reference, the nature of which may now be examined. The framework takes its special form as a result of:

1. A particular value orientation which stems from traditional religious values which have been expanded to form the basis of social work philosophy;

2. A particular conception of the problems confronting modern man in his community and social life; and

3. Certain assumptions that influence method, which derive in part from the value orientation of, and in part from experience in, social work.

15 Importance of Community Organization Practice in Conflict Resolution

> *"Conflict in an ever-present process in human relations"*
> *(Loomis and Loomis, 1965)*

When turning-the-other-cheek fails, many people are at a loss in dealing with conflict. The consensus strategy (a strategy based upon agreement by the total group), employed by many organizations, leaves community leaders ill-prepared to deal with those persons or organizations who refuse to concede without a struggle.

Conflict situations appear with frequency in daily, public, and private life. These conflicts may be on a small or large scale; they may occur within and among groups, communities, or nations; and, they may be triggered by ethnic, racial, religious, or economic differences, or arise from differences in values, beliefs, and attitudes regarding issues. Local communities are constantly faced with issues such as funding for education, siting of waste facilities and zoning that have the potential of leading to community conflict. Workers in community organizations are (or should be) aware of issues and value differences that may cause conflict within or among groups. Unmanaged conflict is a threat to the survival of the group and, at the least, tends to make the group less effective.

What causes conflict to emerge in communities and community groups? How can one minimize, deal with, "manage", or resolve community and group conflict? How is conflict used by groups as a strategy to bring about desired changes? This paper will address these questions and provide a means for individuals who work in voluntary development groups to understand and deal with conflict within and among community groups.

What is Conflict

The potential for conflict exists whenever and wherever people have contact. As people are organized into groups to seek a common goal, the probability of conflict greatly increases. Since only the most serious conflicts make headlines, conflict has a negative connotation for many people. All conflicts are not the same. We face conflicts on all levels (Barker *et al.* 1987). We have disagreements with family, friends, and co-workers. "Conflicts are rarely resolved easily. Most conflicts are managed as individuals work out differences . . ." (Barker *et al.* 1987).

Individuals may dislike certain people with whom they come into frequent contact, but may tolerate their behaviour on a day-to-day basis until a situation arises where strong feelings are at issue. Such situations almost inevitably turn up, sooner or later, within any long term community project or programme. Conflict can occur within groups (intra-group conflict) or among groups (inter-group conflict).

Types of Conflict

Three basic types of conflict will be discussed here: task conflict, interpersonal conflict, and procedural conflict. Group members may disagree about facts or opinions from authorities. The interpretation of evidence may be questioned. Disagreement about the substance of the discussion is called "task conflict". Task conflict can be productive by improving the quality of decisions and critical thinking processes.

Another potential area for conflict is the interpersonal relationships within the organization. The term interpersonal conflict is used to indicate the disagreement that most people call a "personality clash". This "clash" may take the form of antagonistic remarks that relate to the personal characteristics of a group member or disregard any organizational goals to antagonize a particular group member. Conflict of this type is expressed through more subtle nonverbal behaviours. There may be icy stares or, at the other extreme, an avoidance of eye contact. Interpersonal conflict may be inevitable and must be managed for optimal group maintenance.

"Procedural conflict" exists when group members disagree about the procedures to be followed in accomplishing the group goal. New procedures may be formulated and a new agenda suggested. Even the group goal may be modified. Procedural conflict, like task conflict, may be productive (Barker *et al.* 1987).

According to Dahrendorf, at least four conditions are necessary if a conflict situation can be said to exist:

1. There must be sets of individuals exhibiting some level of organization. These could be voluntary groups, religious groups, families, communities, nations, or some other collections of individuals.
2. There must be some level of interaction among group members. Without contact (and communication) there can be no conflict. The contact may merely be propaganda about another people, culture, or group; it need not be personal.
3. There must be different levels of positions to be occupied by group members - a hierarchy of relationships. All individuals cannot occupy the same positions at the same time.
4. There must exist a scarcity of needed or desired resources and a general dissatisfaction among members about how these resources are being distributed. When there is dissatisfaction, conflict can erupt (French 1969, Barker *et al.*, 1987).

Because small group communication acts as a system, no single variable operates in isolation. A change in one variable may produce changes in others. Because the system is continuously changing, a small group could possibly experience more than one type of conflict simultaneously (Knutson and Kowitz 1977).

Conflict and Competition

Although competition is often confused with conflict, there are important differences between the two concepts. U.S. society is based on a tradition of competition in jobs and leisure activities as well as in stress competition. Most competition however, contains the seed for potential conflict.

Conflict and competition have a common root because in each case individuals or groups are usually striving toward incompatible goals. The major difference exists in the form of interference that blocks attainment of the goal.

In competition between groups working toward the same goal, the competitors have "rules" (formal and informal guidelines) that limit what they can do to each other in attempting to reach their goal. Athletic events are examples of organized competition with extensive rules setting forth boundaries of behaviour.

Mack (1969) illustrates the difference between competition and conflict by discussing a foot race: as long as the participants are running without interfering with each other, competition exists. If one runner "pokes his foot between the other fellow's legs," the nature of the interaction has changed and conflict exists (so long as the action is defined by both involved parties as interference and not as an acceptable act under the rules).

Robinson and Clifford (1974) presents the following illustration to clarify the distinction between competition and conflict:

> *If two children decide to set up a lemonade stand on a hot summer day, for instance, competition will exist as long as each party attempts to 'corner the market' with socially acceptable behaviour. 'Advertisement campaigns' might be used to praise the superiority of each party's product. 'Price wars' may be used to get the trade. When one party feels threatened by the competition, he may resort to several other tactics.*

If one competitor goes to the other and suggests forming a cooperative, eliminating high-priced advertising and agreeing on a common price, consensus or cooperation may occur. Conflict occurs if one party reacts by making innuendoes about the other's product, perhaps by suggesting that his lemonade may be harmful, or if he organizes a boycott against his opponent. If one party puts salt in his opponent's sugar supply, destroys his opponent's ice, or turns over his opponent's tables, violence occurs.

Competition is often used as technique to stimulate community groups to action. In Extension, for example, the traditional means of working with groups is on a cooperative basis. Involvement in conflict is generally avoided, and Extension is careful not to "take sides" on issues that could produce community group conflict. However, competition is widely used by this educational agency to motivate different individuals, groups, or communities to strive for the same goal. Incentives, such as awards for beautification and other community achievements, are examples of how competition can be used as an effective motivating tool.

The Dimensions of Conflict

Robinson (1972) identifies the dimensions of conflict as:

1. threats or disputes over territory, whether the boundaries of the territory are physical, social, or work boundaries; and
2. threats to values, goals, and policies, as well as threats to behaviour.

With regard to territory, threats to physical boundaries often involve property disputes or controversy over water resources usage by different groups.

Social territories are involved in establishing access to certain resources. Such organizations as a county club, neo-nazis, or religious orders set limits regarding who can join the group. The boundaries are limited by dues structure, religious affiliation, or value structure. However, fewer groups are legally able to limit social territories based on gender, race, and social class.

Other examples of social boundaries involve the concepts of social distance and norms. The Amish illustrate both concepts. They maintain social distance by dressing differently than others in U.S. society as well as by adhering to different rules of behaviour. Because the Amish are seen as having little direct effect on the larger society, conflict is usually minimal. Bussing of school children to achieve integration, however, is an issue involving social boundaries where the potential for conflict is great. (In this case, it should be pointed out, such social boundaries do exist, whether or not they are considered "right" or justifiable).

Threats to work boundaries may arise over job descriptions. Incompatible or unclear lines of work responsibilities can lead to conflict within organizations. Disputes over work territory may also come about in situations where overlapping services and agencies exist. Jurisdictional disputes over emergency medical service, school districts, law enforcement (local police, county sheriffs, state highway patrol), and political units (townships/cities/county) have potential for conflict.

Groups tend to "protect" their territories and maintain their boundaries by excluding others, rewarding and/or pushing group members for the degree to which they adhere to group norms and defend the territory in question, and by holding ethnocentric beliefs.

Groups may also "tend to believe that their way of thinking and doing things is not only the best but the only right way. This belief that the ways of one's own group are superior to all others, sociologists call ethnocentrism" (Mack 1969). Mack contends that ethnocentrism is an important source of and a contributing factor to the continuity of conflict. In an urbanizing and industrializing world, groups may no longer be as physically and socially isolated as they once were.

Conflict can involve threats to values. Such issues as the environmental concerns, abortion, international trade agreements, and the content of public education may threaten individuals and groups with different value orientations.

Conflict may arise over goals. For example, county residents may differ on how much of the county's budget should be allocated to social services or road repairs. Most conflict is the result of incompatibility of goals. However, there are also conflicts that stem from differences about the means to attain goals. In one community, for example, there was general agreement to establish a community park. Some felt it should be paid for by existing revenue. Others believed a new tax source should be secured. As a result, conflict erupted.

Conflict may concern policies, such as adherence to Environmental Protection Agency (EPA) or Occupational Safety and Health Administration (OSHA) guidelines.

Conflict can also involve threats to behaviour: "When values, policies and goals are changed, when territories are redefined, one must develop new behaviour skills" (Robinson 1972). One recent behavioural change example involves the emerging role of women in all facets of our society.

The Effects of Conflict – Positive Aspects of Conflict

"Not all conflict is bad and not all cooperation is good," according to Robinson (1972). People tend to view conflict as a negative force operating against successful completion of group or community goals. Conflict can be harmful to groups but may also serve some potentially positive functions, depending upon the types of groups within and among which it occurs. Not every type of conflict may benefit groups, and conflict may not serve such functions for all groups (Coser and Rosenberg, 1964). Conflict could be productive and could have positive effects on groups. Three of these positive effects are: improving the quality of decisions, stimulating involvement in the discussion, and building group cohesion.

The integrative and disintegrative effects of conflict are examined in the following paragraphs. Much of the material is summarized from Robinson and Clifford (1974), Coser (1964) and Schaller (in Cox, 1974) and Barker *et al.* (1987).

Defining and sharpening issues is one of the positive functions of conflict among community groups. As sides form on an issue, arguments and positions are clarified, and people can more easily distinguish between two different points of view.

Conflict can improve the quality of decisions. Suppose your group is discussing the issue of "student enrolment at your school". You and another member disagree about the number of students attending your college. What would you do Would you continue affirming your position or would you walk to the telephone and call the registrar's office to request the enrollment information contained in its records? Most group members will look for more information to resolve task conflict. Expression or conflicting news generates need for additional information that is imperative to the decision-making process.

Conflict among groups may increase unity and cohesion within each group as members unite in a common purpose. As Mack (1969) suggests, conflict may define, maintain, and strengthen group boundaries, contributing to the group's distinctiveness and increasing group solidarity and cohesion. He adds:

> *"Conflict promotes the formation of groups . . . Conflict also destroys groups, both in the sense of realignments resulting from shifts in the distribution of power . . . and in the ultimate sense of the extermination of an unsuccessful party to conflict".*

Internal social conflicts which concern goals, values or interests that do not contradict the basic assumptions upon which the relationship is founded tend to be positively functional for the social structure. Such conflicts tend to make possible the readjustment of norms and power relations within groups in accordance with the felt needs of its individual members or sub-groups.

Internal conflicts in which the contending parties no longer share the basic values upon which the legitimacy of the social system rests threaten to disrupt the structure.

One of the most obvious "side effects" of task and procedural conflict is excitement, although some of the feelings generated by conflict may be negative, they are evidence of involvement. That is, a group member may be angry but at least he or she is involved in the group discussion. Thus, a good argument may be an effective antidote to apathy. Individual involvement helps groups become more cohesive.

Conflict may lead to alliances with other groups, creating bonds between loosely structured groups or bringing together different individuals and groups in a community as they unite to fight a common threat. Issues, such as types of books used in public schools, have recently brought diverse individuals and groups together in various communities.

Obviously, building group unity through interpersonal conflict is difficult at times. Suppose, for example, that you become extremely angry during an already heated discussion and call another group member "a turkey". If individual and group trust exists and members do not take remarks as personal rejection, the group can grow through the confrontation. Group members learn that together they can confront even personality clashes and as a group work to solve them.

In the words of Fisher (1980), "The group that fights together stays together." The conflict should be managed, however, before it becomes verbal assault and irreparable damage to individual egos occurs (Barker *et al.* 1987).

Conflict often helps gain recognition for the groups) involved. However, conflict may increase bitterness, alienation, and divisiveness within or among groups and may have long-lasting effects upon future cooperation among individuals and groups holding opposite views. Coleman (1957) cites that "the residuum of past controversy", or the cleavages that exist in a community as a result of past conflicts, have an effect on present and future conflicts.

Conflict within a group can allow dissatisfied members to voice their complaints. And, the group may restructure itself to deal with internal dissension and dissatisfaction. However, conflict within a group often leads to internal tension and disruption. Member's attention may be diverted from the goals of the group to focus on the conflict.

The structure of the group and its degree of tolerance of conflict will affect the results of intra-group dissatisfaction and dissension. Groups that have developed close bonds and whose members feel a great involvement and sense of belonging tend to "play down" or suppress conflict and hostile feelings which may be seen as a threat to the unity of the group. Because of this tendency, feelings of hostility within a group can accumulate and intensify over time. If conflict eventually erupts it may be quite intense. This reaction may occur for two reasons (Coser and Rosenberg 1964):

> *First, because the conflict does not merely aim at resolving the immediate issue which led to its outbreak all accumulated grievances which were denied expression previously are apt to emerge at this occasion. Second, because the total personality involvement of the group members makes for mobilization of all sentiments in the conduct of the struggle...and therefore may threaten the very root of the relationship. Cosner concludes that "the closer the group, the more intense the conflict".*

In groups of individuals who participate only marginally, without involving their total personality, conflict is less likely to be disruptive or destructive. Such groups tend to experience fewer conflicts which guard against the breakdown of consensus. Hostilities do not tend to accumulate when tensions are resolved because "such a conflict is likely to remain focused primarily on the condition which led to its outbreak and not to revive blocked hostility; in this way the conflict is limited to 'the facts of the case" (Coser and Rosenberg 1964). Coser (1964) concludes that the number of conflicts experienced by a group is negatively related to the intensity of those conflicts:

> *However, conflict can also disrupt normal channels of co-operation among various segments of the community. Conflict may result in social change, although "change often occurs without conflict, and conflict does not always produce change" (Schaller, in Cox, 1974).*

Conflict may produce harmful side-effects in addition to the intended change. When teachers strike for higher wages, in a simplified example, students miss several weeks of school work - no matter what the outcome of the strike. A successful bid for wage increases or the death of the teacher's union might be seen as a desirable change by various groups, yet the negative side effect remains in either case.

Conflict may become violent and in extreme cases, lead to destruction and bloodshed. Conflict does not necessarily imply or lead to violence; "conflict becomes violence when the process turns to overt hostility and involves destructive behaviour" (Robinson and Clifford 1974). Conflict may also lead to violence "when a group is forced to change because its rights and privileges have been threatened or usurped" (Robinson 1972).

Clark (1968) states that two conditions help control community conflict and keep it from turning violent: the degree to which people are similar (for example, age, ethnic background, religion, length of residence, organizational ties); and, the degree to which community members have internalized community values, norms, and traditions, resulting from participation in voluntary organizations and involvement in community life.

In summarizing the effects of conflict, it can be said that they are many and varied, as well as unpredictable. In general, conflict may:

- be harmful to individuals or groups;
- have positive results;
- help define and sharpen community issues to improve decisions;
- help gain recognition for a group;
- increase bitterness, alienation, and divisiveness;
- increase unity, cohesion, and solidarity within a group;
- strengthen group boundaries;
- aid in the formation of a new group;
- weaken or destroy a group;
- increase tension within or between groups;
- result in restructuring a group;
- lead to alliances with other groups;
- disrupt normal channels of cooperation; and
- become violent.

As we have seen, conflict has several positive aspects. However, conflict also is potentially destructive in groups when it consumes individual members' energies. However, conflict can interfere with group process and create so much interpersonal hostility that group members may become unwilling or unable to work with one another.

When, Where and Why is Conflict Likely to Occur?

The potential for conflict depends on the degree to which needed resources must be shared, the amount of dependence among individuals and groups, and differences over goals. The "process leading to conflict is dynamic, because of the constantly changing nature of goals" (Schmidt and Kochan 1972). Several specific factors have been related to the occurrence of conflict. Type of event or issue, type of local government, community type, and size will be discussed here.

Type of Event or Issue

Coleman (1957) discusses three components in the development of an event or issue into community conflict:

1. The event must touch upon an important aspect of the community members' lives - education of their children, their means of livelihood, religion, taxes, or something similar.
2. The event must affect the lives of different community members differently. A tax proposal, for example, affects property-owners one way and nonproperty owners another.
3. Finally, the event must be one which community members feel that action can be taken - not one which leaves the community helpless.

Examples of conflict-producing events that fit these descriptions are water quantity, political control of the community, industrialization-related events, books in public school libraries, and other school controversies, including religion in schools and bussing. Coleman (1957) notes that one important difference in the origin of community conflicts is the source: whether they arise internally or are a consequence of external influence. He states that "the prospect for the future is toward an increase in the proportion of externally caused community controversies," since the local community is "less often the focus of important social decisions than it once was".

Coleman (1957) discusses a second difference among the events which produce conflict, the "area of life they affect." The area of life affected might be economic (location of a factory in town, taxes); power or authority (zoning, jurisdictional disputes); cultural values or beliefs (education, fluoridation, religion); and attitudes toward particular persons or groups in the community (a predisposition to react to issues on the basis of who is for or against them).

In discussing the "conditions for controversy," Coleman (1957) cites differences in economic structure (i.e., industrial towns, agricultural towns, etc.); changes in time ("short-term changes in the social climate", such as the violent anti-Communism of the early 1950s); existing cleavages ("the residual of past controversy"); and shifts in population and values (such as rural communities facing an influx of new residents with different values, attitudes and interests, which in turn affect schools, churches, political structure, and taxes). In the future, it seems likely that growth-related issues, such as land use planning, will increase the potential for community conflict.

Schilit (1974) states that "as we move toward revenue sharing conflict in communities will undoubtedly increase." Schilit suggests that as decisions are made over revenue distribution at the local level, there will be increased tension among groups for their "fair" share of resources.

Coleman notes that when issues emerge as conflict they move from the specific to the general. This broadening brings forth new issues as well as new leaders.

Type of Local Government

Gilbert (in Clark 1968) studied power and decision-making in 166 American communities. On the relationship between local government type and conflict, he found that communities with a significantly lower level of conflict were those that had conciliatory values, which facilitated the managing of conflict if it developed. The communities also tended to be more homogeneous in population composition and therefore had fewer internal differences, decreasing the potential for conflict.

Community Type and Size

Regardless of economic base or homogeneity, all communities have the potential for conflict. Level and intensity of conflict has no limitations in any community.

On the relationship between population size and conflict, Gilbert (Clark 1968) states:

> *Although population size is an important factor in conflict - very large cities tend to be those with the most unmanageable conflicts - sheer numbers are not the "cause." Large cities have disproportionately large numbers of persons who are poor and uneducated. These cities are also "over-diversified " economically in that they are national or regional centers of finance, manufacturing, communications, and the like. This differentiation verging on fragmentation seems to contribute to conflict.*

Industrialization and social change in communities affects the potential for conflict. "Industrialization has made possible the rapid interchange of persons and ideas not only within large societies but between societies . . . (This) increases, if only mathematically, the possibility of interpersonal and intergroup friction, both within and between societies" (Mack 1969). As we move toward a "mass society" the possibilities for conflict are increased.

As Parker (1974) notes:

> *"Change, actual or attempted, also results in conflict within a group. There are tendencies to resist change and a fear of the 'unknown' or what might result from changes".*

Some resist change, of course, for more concrete reasons - because their evaluation of the proposed change concluded that it is no improvement.

Understanding Conflict as a Strategy in Social Change

Conflict, as a strategy, is an attempt to coerce power after understanding and reason fail. There are individuals and groups who use conflict as a strategy to achieve their goals and change existing conditions. They may instigate conflict to gain recognition and call attention to their message. They usually want people higher in the power structure to address their problem. In effectively approaching in such situations, it is necessary to understand how conflict can be used as a strategy in social change. One of the necessary "tools" in conflict management is an awareness and understanding of the strategies that agitators use in generating conflict (Robinson and Clifford 1974).

Saul Alinsky was one of the major advocates of using conflict to achieve group goals. His basic strategy was to organize community and neighborhood groups to "establish a creative tension within the establishment" (Robinson and Clifford 1974). Whether the tension was creative or not, tension was frequently "created".

Those who utilize the conflict approach may use disruptive tactics to call attention to their position. These tactics may range from non-violent protests - boycotts and sit-ins - to violence.

Community development professionals appear to be divided on the use of conflict. Steuart (1974), speaking to professionals in the community development field, states: "Conflict itself . . . of some kind or degree is a major determinant of change and far from moving to avoid or immediately dissolve it, it may often be entirely appropriate even to stimulate it." Many reject conflict because they feel that decisions reached through community consensus and cooperation is the best method to achieve social change. Conflict, it is argued, may stimulate participation in the decision making process but provide only a temporary stimulus and prevent the development of a permanent foundation for participation. Many individuals who find conflict distasteful may be repelled (Schaller, in Cox, 1974).

Schaller (in Cox, 1974) states that although benefits often accrue when conflict is properly used, there are risks involved in using conflict in community organizations. Nonviolent conflict may turn violent, and conflict may produce unexpected results. Conflict may also result in the identification of the wrong "enemy". As Robinson and Clifford (1974) notes:

> "Alinsky demonstrated that his approach would bring change. Sometimes his methods generated great unrest and created much stress within communities. At other times, significant advances and social change occurred".

While many community development workers may not promote the use of conflict to bring about change, it is necessary to understand how it may be used by groups in order to deal with conflict situations more effectively when they arise.

Managing Conflict

This final section will discuss approaches to conflict resolution in line with the aim of the discussion - to aid the reader in developing effective skills for coping with conflict.

Robinson and Clifford (1974) advocates "managing conflict toward constructive action since a conflict can seldom be completely resolved." When conflict arises, we need to be able to manage it so that it becomes a positive force, rather than a negative force threatening to disrupt the group or community. As Parker (1974) notes:

> Conflict not managed will bring about delays, disinterest, lack of action and, in extreme cases, a complete breakdown of the group. Unmanaged conflict may result in withdrawal of individuals and an unwillingness on their part to participate in other groups or assist with various group action programmes.

Boulding (1962) discusses several methods of ending conflicts:
1. avoidance;
2. conquest; and
3. procedural resolution of some kind, including reconciliation and/or compromise and/or award.

As stated previously, avoidance of conflict often leads to intensified hostility and may later cause greater problems for the group. Therefore, one of the first steps in conflict management is to recognize that a conflict situation exists. Don't ignore it and count on it disappearing by itself. As Boulding (1962) notes:

> *"The biggest problem in developing the institutions of conflict control is that of catching conflicts young. Conflict situations are frequently allowed to develop to almost unmanageable proportions before anything is done about them, by which time it is often too late to resolve them by peaceable and procedural means."*

Avoidance in a particular situation might conceivably be the best answer, but this step should be made only after conflict is explicitly recognized and alternative ways to manage it are examined.

Conquest or the elimination of all other points of view is an approach seldom applicable to community development programmes. It is mentioned here only as a recognized approach.

Boulding's third method of ending conflict - procedural resolution by reconciliation and/or compromise - is generally the method most appropriate in community development programmes. There are several means to reach a compromise. Various practitioners and academies theorize as to the best means available. In reality, the means for conflict resolution by reconciliation is dependent on the situation. No one type can apply to all situations.

There are always risks involved when dealing with hostilities or conflict. Research indicates that accepting these risks will result, when the conflict is managed (even in varying degrees), in stronger, more cohesive groups. Ignoring or openly fighting the opposition can greatly weaken group structure and group action (Parker 1974).

Compromise involves adjustments and modifications with regard to the territories, values, goals, and/or policies of the involved parties. For example, a possible strategy for reducing conflict over how to reach an agreed-upon goal might be to redefine the situation in terms of new means toward the acceptable goals - a new bond issue rather than depleting existing funds. Territories may also be redefined and made less exclusive in order to diminish conflict.

An outline of suggestions for use in managing conflict within and among community groups is presented below:

1. Recognize and acknowledge that conflict exists.
2. Analyze the existing situation.
   - Know exactly what the conflict is about. Does it involve values, goals, means to goals, territory, or a combination of these?
   - Analyze behaviour of involved parties: members of the groups(s).
   - Determine if the conflict approach is being used by the concerned party (as discussed in previous section).
   - Find out how other, similar conflicts have been resolved.
3. Facilitate Communication.
   - Enhance communication. Open the lines for free discussion and involve all members.
   - Encourage accurate communication and feedback because negotiation (discussed below) depends on good communication.
   - Listen and raise questions.
   - Allow free expression. Constructive disagreement should not be suppressed.
   - Supply information and facts.
   - Maintain an objective level (not emotional).

- Stay on issues, not people.
- Provide the tact needed to "save face" for parties.

4. Negotiate.

"Techniques used in labour disputes offer potential in community problem-solving." (Schilit 1974)

Some useful principles based on negotiations between labour and management, and in business affairs may be applied in conflict management in community groups. As Nierenberg (1968) states, "Whenever people exchange ideas with the intention of changing relationships, whenever they confer for agreement, they are negotiating". He adds, "The satisfaction of needs is the goal common to all negotiations," and that "the satisfaction of needs is the goal common to all negotiations . . . Negotiation is a cooperative enterprise; common interests must be sought; negotiation is a behavioural process, not a game; in a good negotiation, everybody wins something".

The importance of discovering common interests, or "points of common agreement," is stressed by Nierenberg (1968):

Always be on the alert to convert divergent interests into channels of common desires. In exploring these channels, both parties to the negotiation may be stimulated by the idea of sharing common goals. These goals are reached by finding mutual interests and needs by emphasizing the matters that can be agreed upon, and by not dwelling on points of difference.

5. Make necessary Adjustments, Reinforce, Confirm.
6. Live with Conflict. All conflict cannot be resolved.

Sometimes, individuals or groups do not feel it is to their collective interest to resolve a conflict. The price is too high. Resolution involves compromise or capitulation. If a party is unwilling to compromise or to capitulate, then the conflict is likely to continue.

Many social analysts believe that the middle class in Western industrial nations has embraced an anti-conflict, anti-violence value orientation. This has resulted in rule by consensus and conflict avoidance. Some or most community leaders find conflict both embarrassing and distasteful. This attitude is especially useful to those who use a conflict strategy - that is, they exploit peace at any price. But, it may not always be in communities' interest to compromise or capitulate on these terms. Learning to live with conflict may be a real community service. As close knit groups have demonstrated for centuries, communities can live with conflict when they collectively determine it is necessary.

Bibliography

Ardrey, Robert, *The Territorial Imperative*. New York: Atheneum, 1970.

Arthur, Dunham: *Community Welfare Organization, Principles and Practice*, Thomas Y.Crowell Co., New York, 1958, pp. 23.

Barker, Larry L., Kathy J. Wahlers, Kittie W. Watson, Robert J. Kibler, *Groups in Process: An Introduction to Small Group Communication*, Third Edition. Prentice, Hall, Englewood Cliffs, NJ, 1987.

Barry, Mildred C.," Current Concepts in Community Organization", in Group Work and Community Organization, 1956. Paper Presented at the 83rd Annual Forum of National Conference of Social Work, St. Louis, Mo., May 1956, Columbia Press, 1956.

Barry, Mildred. "Community Organization Process", *Social Work Journal*, October 1950, p. 157.

Batten, T.R., *The Human Factor in Community Work*. London: Oxford University Press, 1965.

Beal, George M., Ronald C. Powers and E. Walter Coward, Jr. (Eds.), *Sociological Perspectives of Domestic Develop Meet*. Ames: Iowa State University Press, 1971.

Bennis, Benne and Chin, *The Planning of Change* (Second edition). New York: Holt, Rinehart and Winston, 1969.

Biddle, William and Loureide Biddle, *The Community Development Process: The Rediscovery of Local Initative.* New York: Holt, Rinehart and Winston, 1965.

Bienen, Henry, *Violence and Social Change.* Chicago: University of Chicago Press, 1968.

Black, Algernon D., *The People and the Police.* New York: McGraw-Hill Company, 1968.

Blizek, William L. and Jerry Cederblom, "Community Development and Social Justice." *Journal of the Community Development Society,* Vol. 4, No. 2, 4552, 1973.

Boehm, Werner W., The Nature of Social Work:, Social Work III (April 1958). Carter, Genevieve W., *Practice Theory in Community Organization, Social Work* III (1958).

Boulding, Kenneth E., *Conflict and Defense, A General Theory.* New York: Harper Torchbooks, Harper and Row, Publishers, 1962.

Cassidy, Florence G., *"Principle of Community Organization"* in Harper, E.B. and Dunham, Arthur (eds.)

Clark, Terry N. (Ed.), *Community Structure and Decision Making: Comparative Analyses.* San Francisco: Chandler Publishing Company, 1968.

Coleman, James S., *Community Conflict.* New York: The Free Press (monograph), 1957.

Collier, Peter (Ed.), *Crisis—A Contemporary Reader.* New York: Harcourt, Brace and World, Inc., 1969.

Cook, James B., *Compromise, Conflict and Perspective.* Department of Regional and Community Affairs, College of Public and Community Services, University of Missouri, Columbia, 1975.

Coser, Lewis A. and Bernard Rosenberg, *Sociological Theory: A Book of Readings* (Second Edition). New York: The Macmillan Company, 1964.

Cox, Fred M., *et al.* (Eds.), *Strategies of Community Organization, A Book of Readings.* Itasca, Illinois: F.E., Peacock Publishers, Inc., 1974.

Dayal, Parameshwari: *Gandhian Approach to Social Work*, Gujarat Vidyapith, Ahmedabad, 1986.

Dunham, Arthur. "The Outlook for Community Development — An International Symposium, *International Review of Community Development*, v (1960).

Ehrenreich, Barbara and John Ehrenreich, *The American Health Empire*. New York: Vintage Books, 1971.

Etzioni, Amitai and Eva Etzioni, *Social Change*. New York: Basic Books, 1964.

Finley, James R. and Anthony A. Hickey, *A Study of Water Resource Public Decision Making. Technical Report 37*, 1971.

Fisher, B.A., *Small Group Decision Making: Communication Group Process*, Second Edition. NY: McGraw-Hill, 1980.

Fisher, Ronald J. and James H. White, "A Prescriptive Model: Intergroup Conflicts Resolved by Outside Consultants." *Journal of the Community Development Society*, Vol. 7, No. 1, 1976.

Foster, George M., *Traditional Cultures and the Impact of Technological Change*. New York: Harper and Brothers, 1962.

French, Robert Mills (Ed.), *The Community—A Comparative Perspective*. Itasca, Illinois: F.E. Peacock Publishers, Inc., 1969.

Gamson, William A., "Rancorous Conflict in Community Politics." In: *The Search for Community Power*, Hawley, Willis D. and Frederick M. Wirt (Eds.). Englewood Cliffs, New Jersey: Prentice-Hall Inc., 1968.

Gittell, Marilyn, *Demonstration for Social Change - An Experiment in Local Control*. New York: Institute for Community Studies, Queens College of the City University of New York, 1971.

Goodenough, Ward Hunt, *Cooperation in Change*. New York: Russell Sage Foundation, 1963.

Gurr, Ted with Charles Ruttenberg, *The Conditions of Civil Violence: First Tests of a Casual Model*. Princeton University: Center of International Studies. Research, Monograph No. 28, 1967.

Havens, A. Eugene, "Methodological Issues in the Study of Development." Paper Presented to the Third World Congress of Rural Sociology, Baton Rouge, Louisiana, 1972.

Hawley, Willis D. and Frederick M. Wirt (Eds.), *The Search for Community Power*. Englewood Cliffs, New Jersey: Prentice-Hall, Inc., 1968.

Huizer, Gerrit, *The Utilization of Conflict in Community Development and Peasant Organization: A Case from Chile*, 1970.

Johns, Roy and Demarche, David F., *Community and Agency Responsibility*, New York: Association Press, 1951.

Knutson, T.J. and A.C. Kowitz, "Efforts of Informational Type and Level of Orientation on Consensus Achievement in Substantive and Affective Small Group Conflict." *Central States Speech Journal*, 1977; 28, 5463, 1977.

Kramer, Ralph M. and Harry Specht, *Readings in Community Organization Practice*. Englewood Cliffs, New Jersey: Prentice-Hall, Inc., 1969.

Lippet, Ronald, Jeanne Watson and Bruce Westley, *The Dynamics of Planned Change*. New York: Harcourt, Brace and World, Inc., 1969.

Loomis, Charles P. and Zona K. Loomis, *Modern Social Theories*. Princeton: D. Van Nostrand Company, Inc., 1965.

Mack, Raymond W., "The Components of Social Conflict," In: *Readings in Community Organization Practice*, Ralph M. Kramer and Harry Specht (Eds.). New Jersey: PrenticeHall, Inc., 1969, pp. 327-337.

McNeil, C.F. " Community Organization for Social Work" In: *Social Work Year Book, 1951*, New York: American Association of Social Workers, 1951, p. 123.

McNeil, C.F., Community Organization for Social Welfare, In: *Social Work Year Book*, 1951-54. pp. 122-123.

Minsky, Saul D., *Reveille for Radicals*. Chicago: University of Chicago Press, 1946.

Murray, Ross, *Community Organization—Theory and Principles*, Harper Bros., New York, 1955.

Nierenberg, Gerard I., *The Art of Negotiating*. New York: Hawthorn Books, Inc., 1968.

Parker, John, "Some Ideas About Working With People Individually and in Groups." Ohio Cooperative Extension Service, 1974.

Rao, K. Mukund,*"Community Organization"*, Planning Commission: Encyclopedia of Social Work in India, Volume One, 1968.

Robert, Moriis and Robert Binstok, *Feasible Planning for Social Change*, Columbia University Press, New York, 158.

Robinson, Jerry W., Jr., "The Management of Conflict." *Journal of the Community Development Society*, Vol. 3, No. 2, pp. 100-105, 1972.

Robinson, Jerry W., Jr. and Roy A. Clifford, "Conflict Management in Community Groups." University of Illinois at Urbana-Champaign, *North-Central Regional Extension Publication* No. 36-5, 1974.

Robinson, Jerry W., Jr., Roy A. Clifford and Jake DeWalle, "Stress in Community Groups." University of Illinois at Urbana-Champaign, *North-Central Regional Extension Publication* No. 36-9, 1975.

Ronald, Lippitt, J Watson and B. Westly, *The Dynamics of Planned Change, A Comparative Study of Principles and Technique*, Harcourt, Brace and Co., New York, 1958.

Ross, Murray and Ben Lappin, *Community Organization: Theory, Principles and Practice*. New York: Harper and Row, 1967.

Ross, Murray G., *Community Organization – Theory and Principles*, New York, New York: Harper and Brothers, 1955, p. 39.

Ross, Murray G., *Conceptual Problems in Community Organization*. In: *The Social Services*, Chicago: June, 1956, p. 180.

Sanderson, D. and Polson R.A., *Rural Community Organization*, New York: John Wiley and Sons, 1939, Quoted by M.R. Ahmad. p. 138.

Schilit, Henrietta, "Coping with Community Crisis: New Rules, New Roles for Conflict Resolution." *Journal of the Community Development Society*, Vol. 5, No. 2, 1974.

Schmidt, Stuart M. and Thomas A. Kochan, "Conflict: Toward Conceptual Clarity." *Administrative Science Quarterly*, 1972.

Sherif, Muzafer et al., *Intergroup Conflict and Cooperation—The Robbers Cave Experiment*. Norman, Oklahoma: Institute of Group Relations, The University of Oklahoma, 1961.

Siddiqui, H.Y: *Working with Communities an Introduction to Community Work*, Hira Publications, New Delhi, 1997.

Soodan, K.S. *An Introduction to Social Work Theory and Practice: Community Organization*, Navjyoti Simranjeet Publication pp. 319.

Steiner, Frederick Jesse: *Community Organization*, The New Century Co. New York 1958.

Steuart, Guy W., "Conflict, Social Justice and Neutrality—A Critique and an Alternative." *Journal of Community Development Society*, Vol. 5, No. 1, 1974.

Stinchcombe, Arthur L., *Constructing Social Theories*. New York: Harcourt, Brace and World, 1968.

Thullen, Manfred, "Alternative Approaches to Development." Paper Presented at the North Central Region Intensive Training Programme for Non-Metropolitan Development, 1975.

United Nations, *Principles of Community Development*, Excerpted from Social Progress Through Community Development, 1955.

Walton, Richard E. and John M. Dutton, "The Management of Interdepartmental Conflict: A Model and Review." *Administrative Science Quarterly*.

Warren, Roland L., *The Community in America* (Second Edition). Chicago: Rand McNally College Publishing Company, 1972.

Weeks, D. *The eight essential Steps to Conflict Resolution: Preserving Relationships at Work at Home, and in the Community*. Los Angeles: J.P. Tarcher (1972).

Whiting, Larry R. (Ed.), *Communities Left Behind: Alternatives for Development*. Ames: The Iowa State University Press, 1974.

Wileden, Arthur F., *Community Development*. Totowa, New Jersey: Bedminister Press, 1970.

Wilson, James Q., *Varieties of Police Behaviour*. Cambridge: Harvard University Press, 1969.

Wise, H.F. and J.B. Williams, Editors, *Main Street Ohio: Opportunities for Bringing People Back to Downtown*. State of Ohio: Department of Development (1981).

Walter, A. Friendlander and Robert Z. Apte: *Introduction to Social Welfare*, Prentice-Hall India Private Limited, 1982.

Index

A

Advocacy, 49
American Association for Community Organization (AACO), 23
American Red Cross, 25

B

Basic steps in community organization, 67-69
  action plan, 68
  beneficiaries profile, 68
  building counter system, 69
  determination of strategy, 68
  identifying the problem, 67
  implementation and evaluation, 69
  linking people with the programme, 69
  perception of the problem, 67
  structural-functional analysis, 68
Basis of race or sex, 44
Buffalo, 22

C

Characteristics and skills of a good community organizer, 45-48
Characteristics of a good organizer, 45
  curiosity, 45
  discerning and critical eye, 46
  free and open mind, 46
  imagination, 45
  irreverence, 45
  organized personality, 46
  receptive ear, 46
  sense of humour, 45
Charity Organization Society, 22, 27
Cincinnati Public Health Federation, 23
Community, 3
Community Chests and Councils of America, 23
Community organization, 5
  common objectives, 7
  community organization as a problem-solving method, 10-12
  community organization as macro method of practice in social work, 10
  methods and procedures of community organization, 12-13
  philosophy of community organization, 6-7
  secondary objectives, 7-9
  value assumptions, 9-10
Community organization in UK

first phase, 26
fourth phase, 26
second phase, 26
third phase 1950 onwards, 26
Community Welfare Councils, 23
Conflict, 101-103
Current issues in community organization, 81-86
   allocation of roles, 83
   axis of inequality of caste and class, 85
   caste as a unit and as a system, 84-85
   caste, 85
   class, 86
   elements of the gender system, 83-84
   gender sensitive community organization practice, 82-83
   gender-based hierarchical placement, 83
   male-female differentiation, 83

D

Democratic procedures, 70
Democratic system of values, 3
Development of leadership, 71

E

Educational aspects, 71
Environmental Protection Agency, 106

F

Federal Security Agency, 24

G

Gandhi, 30
Gandhian approach to community organization, 30
Generic Community Welfare Organization, 24

H

History of community organization in India, 27-30
   difference between community organization and community development, 29-30
   Gandhian approach to community organization, 30
History of community organization in UK and USA, 21-26
   charity organization period 1870-1917, 22-23
   community organization in UK, 25
   history of community organization, 22
   period of expansion and professional development from 1935 to present time, 24-25
   rise of federation (1917 to 1935), 23
   why should we study history, 21

I

Imagination, 45
Importance of community organization practice in conflict resolution, 100-120
   what is conflict, 101
   types of conflict, 101-103
   conflict and competition, 103-104

Index

dimensions of conflict, 104-106
effect of conflict-positive aspects of conflict, 106-111
when, where and why is conflict likely to occur, 111-112
type of event or issue, 112-113
type of local government, 113
community type and size, 114
managing conflict, 116-120
understanding conflict as a strategy in social change, 114-116

Institutions, 2

J

Juvenile delinquency, 30

L

Lane Committee, 7
Location of community work in the context of social work, 14-20
Location of community work within social work, 16
   concept of community analysis, 17
   horizontal components, 17-19
   vertical components, 19-20
London Charity Association, 22
London Society, 22

M

Meaning, definition and basic assumptions of community organization, 1-13
Models and approaches of community organization, 58-66
   approaches to community organization, 64
   model, 58

model A - locality development, 59
model B - social planning, 59-60
model C - social action, 60
models of community organization by Rothman, 58-59
models of Rothman, 60-61
neighbourhood development model, 61-62
neighbourhood organizing, 64
   social work approach, 64-65
   political activists approach, 65
   neigbourhood maintenance/ community development approach, 65-66
structural change model, 63-64
system change model, 62

N

National Conference of Social Work, 7, 24
NGOs, 28, 62

O

Occupational Safety and Health Administration, 106
Organizer acts, 49
Oxford Dictionary, 82

P

Participatory Rural Appraisal, 88
Principles of community organization, 32
   active and vital participation, 36

clear identification of the community, 34-35
communities right of self determination should be respected, 36-37
community organization is means and not an end, 34
community organization is to promote community solitary and the practice of democracy, 34
continual participatory evaluation, 38
dynamic and flexible nature of programmes and services, 38
fact-finding and needs assessment, 35
identification, mobilization and utilization of the available resources, 35
limited use of authority or impulsion, 38
participatory planning, 35-36
recognition and involvement of indigenous leadership, 37-38
spirit of cooperation rather than competition, and the practice of coordination of effort, 37
voluntary cooperation, 37
Principles of community organization practice, 31-38
Problems, 2

R

Relevance of community organization in community development, 70-74

distinction between community organization and community development, 72-73
working with individuals, families, and groups within the community, 73-74
Role of a social worker in community organization practice, 49-57
advocate, 55
animator, 51-52
catalyst, 54-55
collaborator, 53 consultant, 53
communicator, 50
counselor, 52-53
critical level of consciousness, 57
educator, 56
empowerment, 57
enabler, 51
facilitator, 55
guide, 52
innovator, 53-54
level of consciousness, 56
magic level of consciousness, 56
mediator, 56
model, 54
motivator, 54
naïve level of consciousness, 57
Rosenberg, 109
Ross, Murray G., 2

S

Self-help, 71
Sense of humour, 45
Settings of community organization practice in social work, 87-99

Index

community welfare planning, 94-96
continuation, 94
evaluate the action, 94
formulate achievable objective, 91-92
give priorities, 90
implement the plan of action, 93
list the problems, 90
mobilization of resources, 93
modification, 94
principles of planning, 96-97
redefine the problem, 91
select a problem, 91
select an appropriate alternative, 92
select the next problem, 94
social action, 87-90
three contrary views. 97-98
value assumptions, 98-99
work out the alternatives, 92
work out a plan of action, 93

Skills of an effective community organizer, 46
conflict resolution, 47
networking, 47
organizing meeting, 47
problem analysis, 46
resource mobilization, 47
training, 48
writing reports, 47

Social interaction, 1
Social Service Exchange, 23

T

Third International Survey, 13

U

Understanding power in the context of community organization, 75-80
barriers of empowerment, 79-80
concept of power, 75
dimensions of power, 75-77
relevance of power in community organization, 78-79

United Nations, 5
USA, 14

V

Values and ethics of community organization practice, 39-44
Voluntary cooperation, 71

W

Work out a plan of action, 93
Work out the alternatives, 92
World War I, 16, 23
World War II, 24

HONDSEGEDAGTE

AFRIKAANS

Arme hond. Hy sluip hier rond terwyl ons
die brood moet breek. Hy beloer jou met
sy kop omlaag, die hond. Hy dink hy sal
'n krummel kry as dié ooit val, maar dis
verniet, die arme fokken hond. Dit klou
aan 'n nat vinger en rol op jou eie mond

Die brood moet breek, want ons is bleek
van honger. Arme hond. 'n Klontjie botter
is 'n droom vanuit 'n ander tyd, toe ons
nog almal jonger was, arme hond. Nou
breek ons die brood op, skraap dit in vet
van laasweek, al is dit ongesond

Arme hond. Hy grawe in die grond. Harde
bene om te kou, maar dit maak vir lekker
sop: Dun is die water, en as hy tjank, help
'n goed-gemikte skop, die arme hond.
Hy sluip eers weg, kom kruip dan terug,
reuke op sy snoet van ander stront

Hy lê by ons voete, die arme fokken
hond. Hy lek aan ons vingers, dit help
om hul skoon te hou. Hy druk sy snoet
onder jou hand in, die hond. Hy lek
aan sy pote, hy byt in sy lieste, jeuk en
byt en word een groot fokken wond

HANS PIENAAR

DOG THOUGHTS

Poor dog. He prowls about while we
must break the bread. He ogles you with
his head held low, this dog. He thinks he'll
scout a crumb that falls, but it's all
for nought, the poor fucking dog. It clings
to a wet finger, and into your mouth it rolls.

The bread must break, because we are pale
with hunger. Poor dog. A pat of butter's
a dream from another time, when we
were all younger, poor dog. Now we
break the bread apart, scrape it in last
week's fat, though it's quite unfit.

Poor dog. He's digging a hole. Hard
bones to chew, but they make tasty
soup: The water's thin, and when he whines,
a well-placed kick does the job, poor dog.
He cowers away, then cowers back,
his snout smells of other shit.

He lies at our feet, the poor fucking
dog. He licks our fingers, it keeps
them clean. He jostles his snout under
your hand for more, the dog. He licks
his paws, he bites his loins, itches and
bites and becomes one big fucking sore.

Translated from the Afrikaans original – Hans Pienaar's
Hondsegedagte – by Pieter Odendaal

BATJHA

Sesotho

Batjha le ya kae le potlakile?
Ha lebone tsela empa tsatsi letjhabile.
Tshwarang letie le sa le tjhabetse,
Holang, lethenthetse le sa le tjhabetse.

Motjha nako e o file ona marapo,
Nako ya ho kgaba eseng ho robala malopo.
Tsetlallelang ho tswella le sa na le nako,
Le kgabeng pele le fetoha dithako.

Tsatsi ha le se tjhabe le sa paqame,
Hoba e tlang ke nako, e tla e palame,
Nako haena ena abuti kapa motswala,
Motjha tsoha e fihlile nako ya ho sela.

Motjha tlase lefatsheng mona o morumuwa,
Pheta ditaelo jwale ka yena mothoduwa.
Hoba nako le metsotso ya botjha ba motho,
Ha e kodumela e ba yona tshomo-ka-mathetho.

Telang timiti le tele le ona masawana,
Le be matjato a ho tsoha ka madungwane.
Tshwarang ka matla le sa tjhabile,
Ha le dikela o tsebe ho fedile.

Ha le dikela ohle o lebale,
Hobane ho kgutla ha le kgutle lekgale.
Lefatsheng lemo tsa botjha ba motho,
Dintle empa ha di kodumela eba ke phetho.

Motjha akga diala o tone mahlo,
Hoba le ka kwano le meutlwa le ditshehlo.
Le lekgonatha le batla motho a bohlale,
Kgaba ka mathata motjha obe seemahale.

SEHLOHO PIET RAMPAI

GENERATION X

Generation X where are you going in such haste?
You don't see the way yet the sun is fully bright.
Be hands on when you still can,
Grow, have fun while the sun is still bright.

Generation X time has given you a chance,
Time to shine and don't go astray.
Strive while there is still time,
Succeed in excellence before all fades away.

Make means and efforts while you still can,
For the time will come, it's upon us.
Time knows no gender nor relation,
Generation X wake up and make it happen.

Generation X you are on Earth for a purpose,
Do your part as a bearer of good,
For the time of youth does fade away.
When the clock strikes so shall you.

Do away with senseless behavioural culture,
Be that early bird that catches the fat worm at dawn.
Hang on tight while you still can,
For the time is no longer on your side.

Lost time cannot be recovered,
Every second counts, can never be the same as the next.
Time is precious and should be cherished by all,
The fruits of youth should be cherished while ripe.

Generation X build that empire with your might,
For your path is narrow and full of thorns.
Be wise lest you be consumed by greed and envy,
Shine bright and be the legend.

Translated from the Sesotho original – Sehloho Piet Rampai's Batjha – by Goodenough Mashego

LABELS

ENGLISH

I am a positive nihilist.
A spectrophobic, autophobic, catastrophic thinker.
A heterosexual sapiosexual
With some bisexual leanings.
(Love me).

I am an atheistic Jewish girl,
So I think and write a lot.
I am an onychophagic, trypanophobic existentialist.
A follower of fashion from the 1980s
Attempting to be body positive.
(See me).

I am a socialist with a dash of practical capitalism,
An anti-classist semi-Marxist,
An anti-racist semi-artist,
A generally generous idealist
With some logical leanings.
(Hear me).

I am tired of labels.

JULIETTE ROSE-INNES

FAITH

ENGLISH

I am tear-stained and grass-stained
when she picks me up from school.
As I get into the car, I hide the graze on my elbow
but I relay word-for-word the details of the scrap.
How I defended their honour. Swore they'd never lie.
As we drive from the car park, I am a small fuming zealot.
Adamant. Declaiming. Undaunted.

An intervention is clearly necessary.
So, before she washes my face or feeds me lunch,
she takes me quietly straight from the car to the study,
shuts the door, holds my hands,
tells the truth.
There is no Father Christmas.

"He's really make-believe?"
"He's really make-believe."

I stare through the window as she talks on.
Out in the garden my little sister
draws her Miss Piggy muppet puppet by one leg
over the sun-filled lawn.
She's singing a tune she just made up.

I cry again but nod, agree.
We will keep up the pretence a little while longer, at home.
For her sake.

I look out at her as she hums over the flowerbeds.
She is happy and faraway on the other side of the glass.
But this will happen to her too.

In the weeks that follow, I double my scrutiny.
If they could lie about this?

This Jesus, then?
He can really hear them?
All my thoughts?

DEBORAH SEDDON

O SWELE MPHATO

SEPEDI

šo lehono o gapa tše tšhweu fela
hlogo e hupile morodi
o be a phemela naga bjalo ka mohlabani
mola bangwe ba hlwetše maaka le meratha

ke tate!
ditsebe ga di sa kwa
bošego ga a robale
o tshwenya ke sepoko
meno o šina a sa fetše
o re go bolela, a buše a ikarabe

mefoma ya angola le swaziland di mo onaditše
mokokotlo o gana go otlolloga
gago tema ntle le lehlotlo
mengwaga ke ye masomehlano
ruri ke tša batho!

meraba e a dutla
bana ba gomišwa dikolong
ka baka la mokitlana
go a pala
mphiwafela o a itatola boka ditaola
di šitile phaahle
ebile o gafa ntahle

aforika-borwa ye mpsha
e lokollotšwe bokgobeng
kgoro ya therešo le poelano e kgaotše tshele
koša re sa bina e tee

muši wa tokologo o sa foka
letswai nameng
legare phokeng

14 ya mengwaga robben-island
o ile a kgoketšwa ka diketane
a botoga direthe di palegile
ka malala-a-kwaetše
kgopolo e šila menatla
o bonetše bagale
ba re go galefa
ba mo gaya ntaka ka legare
ruri o di bone dikoma

lehono ba gorogile bagale/adi
bo mandela, sisulu, kathrada le bangwe
mmušo o ba hlakeletše ka diketekete
ge e le tate ya lešidi a hlokišwa
ge e le tše dingwe re boifa go di laodiša
re tšhaba baditi le meretlwa

a gona taba
ge e le koma e alogile
aforika-borwa ke ngwana yo a lokollotšwego popelong
e tswetšwe ka lefsa
yo a sa rego šatee, o a duma!

                          MOSES SELETISHA

THE INITIATION SCHOOL WENT UP IN FLAMES

Today you walk with difficulty
A bullet pierced your skull
You were protecting the country like a warrior
While others were lying and feasting

My father
He can no longer hear
He can't sleep at night
He has nightmares
He gnashes his teeth non-stop
He answers his own questions; talking to himself

caves in swaziland and angola damaged him
He cannot straighten his spine
He can't walk without a stick
He is only fifty
This is witchcraft!

He is broke
His children get evicted from schools
He cannot settle his debts
It's hopeless
He's too young for pension
No one helps him
He's losing his mind

New south africa
Has been freed from slavery
Truth and reconciliation commission ended hostilities
We are still singing the same song

There's still liberation smoke in the air
Peace
Relax

14 years on robben island
He was shackled in chains
arrived heels bleeding
Pierced by thorns
Your mind grinding
You saw secrets of warriors
When they got angry
They shaved his head with a razor
Indeed you saw dark secrets

today s/heroes have returned
mandela, sisulu, kathrada and others
government thanked them with thousands
while my father received nothing
we are afraid to relate other tales
we are afraid of what might come of us

it's fine
that you graduated from initiation
south africa is a child freed from the womb
has been born again
he who does not ululate is jealous

Translated from the Sepedi original – Moses Seletisha's O Swele Mphato – by Goodenough Mashego

HAZARDS

ENGLISH

We hold storms on our tongues,
Every day.

We walk past the streets like tornadoes,
Raging.

Our palates are wrathful skies,
Perplexed
thrusting our tongues to create lightning
in our mouth

Our gums are volcanic eruptions,
Shaking
ready to release the molten voice of our words

We overflow on everyone
as hot as we are;
always aimed to claim everything

We have drowned many of us
in rivers they sucked through their ears.

We layed mountains on tombstones,
for dreams
Never to wake up in calls of resurrection.

We are known for no good but destruction,
to turn our lives into hazards.

NKWANA JOSHUA SERUTLE

OBAB' ABANGEBABA

ISIZULU

Yaqonda ngqo kim' intokazi
Intokaz' owuwangafung' uth' uzime.
Yanyathela kabili kathathu maqede yamoyizela.
Yatshikizis' umzimba phambi kwami
Wen' owabon' onobuhle bekhiph' amakhono
Kimina kwaqubuk' uthand' olubabazekayo
Ngakhumbul' ukuthi ngake ngaba yinsizwa.
Cha, angikhuzelanga; sasingasekh' isidingo
Ngahlal' odabeni funa ngiphunyukwe yiqatha.

Yangithi laphalazi ngamehlo amhlophe qwa
Yashay' isikhwehlela yase ithi,
"Mina nginguNtombenhle
Ngizalwa kwaSokhela
NgingowakwaMkhiz' eMakhabeleni.
Laph' eGoli ngiziphilisa ngokuthengisa ngomzimba."
Kwashwaban' ulimi; ngakhuluma okuzwakalayo
    nokungezwakali
Yize kwafik' umqondo wokuthi ngiqhel' eduze kwayo,
Amahlon' angithi ngqi! Ngema phuhle!

Yaqhubeka yathi, "Ungazikhohlisi uthi ubona intombi
Min' angiyon' intombi,
Min' angikaze ngibe yintombi,
Min' angisoze ngaba yintombi
Noma ngabe ngifisa kangakanani,
Wen' ubon' umfanekiso wentombi
Min' obam' ubuntombi ngabephucwa ngobaba
Obab' abangebon' obaba ngoba bebaba.
Obab' ababezwana nomama bangidlwengula bephindelela."

Zagcwal' emehlweni' izinyembez' entokazini
Yaqale yazam' ukuzibamb' ngezinkophe
Ekugcineni zageleza ngemisedlan' emibili
Imisedlan' engafunda kwezami;
Yayidalwe yikh' ukuhlal' ikhala.
Yazesula yas' ithi, "Ngisengumntwan' angibonanga cala
Mina ngangithi yint' eyenziwa yibo bonk' obaba.
Langa limbe ngamazis' umama
Kwab' ukwehlukana kwabo."

Yaqhuba yathi, "Wamthol' umam' omuny' ubaba.
Kwaqala kwaba kuhle saba ngumndeni
Ubaba waqal' ukungithint' amabele
Lokhu wab' ekwenz' um' umam' engekho
Wayekwenza lokh' elandelisa ngamazwi,
Wayethi ngimuhle ngifana nomama
Njalo uma engibona ngangimkhumbuz' umama.
Angiwuvumelang' umqond' owawuth' angilubik' udaba."

Yaqhuba yathi, "Umshado kamama wokuqala wachithwa yimi
Umshado kamama wesibili wawuzochithwa yimi
Ubaba wayelala nami ngenkani mihla nezolo
Wayethembisa ukungibulala uma ngike ngathi vu.
Mina ngafa ngiphila; ngapoka ngiphila.
Ekugcineni ngasithath' isinqumo
Isinqum' esangehlukanisa nomama
Umam' engimthandayo; umama ozwana nabahlukumezi
Ngalifuthel' ikhay' elalingihlukumeza."

Ukuzibika kwam' okwavusel' intokaz' amanxeba
Kwaphazamiseka lapho kum' imoto kanokusho stopped by
Yama maqeda kwavulek' ifasitela lomshayeli.
Yathi jeq' intokazi yas' ivalelisa kimi.
Yathi, "Ngicela sehlukane yiklanyente lami lel' elimayo."
Angazanga noma kwakumele ngivalelise yini.
Ngama khimilili ngalubuk' unyanyavu lunyelela.
Ngesikade ngazizwa sengikhuluma ngedwa okohlanya,
"Yonk' int' eyenzekayo yenzeka ngesizathu."

        BUKELANI MMELLY SHANGASE

FATHERS WHO ARE NOT FATHERS

The lady came directly onto me
The lady that you would swear was a beauty pageant.
She stepped twice thrice and thereafter smiled
She swayed her body in front of me
As beauty pageants do
In me there grew rapidly the kind of love beyond description
I remembered that I once was a young man.
No I did not propose there was not need
I simply stated my matter as I did not want to miss this opportunity.

She eyed me with those extra white eyes
She cleared her throat and then she said,
"My name is Ntombenhle, The Beautiful one
I am a daughter of Sokhela
I am of the Mkhize clan from eMakhabeleni.
Here in Johannesburg, I survive through selling my body."
I was tongue-tied; what I said next made and did not make sense
Even though there was a nagging idea that I should stay away from here,
I was embarrassed to do so! I stood motionless!

She went on to say, "Don't fool yourself and think that you see a maiden;
I am not a maiden,
I have never been a maiden,
I will never be a maiden
Even though I can wish it with all my heart

You are only seeing an image of a maiden
My maidenhood was taken away from me by fathers
Fathers who were not fathers because they lacked integrity
Fathers who were in love with my mother raped me
    repeatedly."

Her eyes welled up with tears
She attempted to hold them back with her eyelashes
In the end they simply formed two furrows and flowed
    down
These furrows I learnt for myself;
Were formed by constant crying.
She wiped her tears off and said, "While still a child I did
    not see anything wrong
I thought this was what was done by all fathers.
One day I told mother about this
And that was their separation."

She continued and said, "Mother found another man.
Initially all was well. We were a family
Things went awry when I became an adolescent
Father started touching my breasts
He did this when mother was not around,
He usually did this and thereafter said
I am beautiful, I resemble my mother
That every time he sees me I remind him of my mother.
I did not agree with the idea that I should tell about this
    thing."

She went on to say "Mother's first marriage was ruined by

me
And mother's second marriage will also be ruined by me
Father had sex with me forcefully frequently
He promised to kill me if I said anything.
I died alive and haunted alive
In the end I took a decision
A decision that separated me from mother
The mother I love, the mother who loves rapists
I turned my back from a home that was molesting me."

It is my talk about love to her that dug up wounds in the young lady
The conversation was disrupted when a flashy car stopped by
It stopped and then the driver's window was opened.
The lady took one look and bid me farewell.
And said, "I bid you to go, this is my client that has just stopped."
I did not know whether I had to bid her farewell too.
I stood fixed at a spot as I looked on as the flashy car slowly drove away.
After a long pause I heard myself talking alone like a mad man,
"Everything that happens, does so because of a reason."

Translated from the Zulu original – Bukelani Mmelly Shangase's Obab' Abangebaba – by Dr Innocentia Jabulisile Mhlambi

KONAKELEPHI?

IsiZulu

Zehla kwamanz' izifuba kwabesifazane
Kwashintsh' amath' emilonyen' ababa ha
Bakhihl' esikaNandi ngezwe lokhokho
Izwe lokhokh' elalisosizini lwengcindezelo
Sasisikhul' isililo somame besililo.
Ulaka lwalubhalw' emehlwen' emadodeni
Izingane zazishesha emigwaqweni
Kukhona okwakumele kulungisiwe.
Sekwedlule lokh' sesikhululekile
Inyamazane seyibanjiwe kumele yabiwe
Esikhundleni sokuthi yabiwe ngononina
Silibel' ukubhekana ngeziqu zamehlo.
Siyahamb' isikhath' asimele thina
Siyogcin' ngokuyidla ngephunga.

BUKELANI MMELLY SHANGASE

WHERE DID IT GO WRONG?

Chests fell like rain among women
Saliva changed in the mouth and became bitter
There was an outcry – just as when the Zulus cried at
    Nandi's death – about the land of our ancestors
The land of our ancestors which at one time was besieged
    by suppression
The outcry was loud, the outcry from mothers' unions
Anger was written on the eyes of the men
Children were walking fast on the streets
There was something that needed to be corrected
That has gone past now we are now free
The game has been caught it must be shared
Instead of it being shared equally amongst everyone
We are now glaring at each other in evil ways
While time passes by without waiting for us
We will eventually only smell the flavours

*Translated from the Zulu original – Bukelani Mmelly Shangase's
Konakelephi? – by Dr Innocentia Jabulisile Mhlambi*

IZIZUKULWANE

IsiZulu

Ukhokho wakhononda ngomkhulu,
Umkhulu wakhononda ngobaba;
Ubab' uyakhononda ngami.
Ubab' uth' akaphendulwa yingane
Asekushilo yena kumele kwenziwe.
Kanti konakala kusiphi isizukulwane?
Isizukulwane ngasinye sisol' esisilandelayo?
Kumele kulungiswen' ukuze kulunge?

Mina ngibon' ikusas' eliqhakazile;
Abangikhulisayo bathi bayoyicel' ivuthiwe
Engikwenzay' abangikhulisayo abakuthandi
Bathi bona babengenzi njengami,
Bathi bona babebahlonipha abazali babo,
Bathi min' angibahloniphi bona,
Bathi mina ngifun' izizathu zabakushoyo,
Bathi mina ngilalel' abangani kakhulu.

Kanti nguban' okumele ngimlalele?
Kanti lincike kuban' ikusasa lami?
Kanti nguban' owazi ngekusasa lami?
Abangikhulisayo bayakwaz' okwayizolo;
Abangikhulisay' abakwaz' okwakusasa;
Okwayizol' akufani nokwakusasa.
Kant' uban' owaz' okumele kwenziwe
Ukuze kuhlangatshezwane nekusasa?

Bazali bethu sikhululeni sizibonele;
Enisihlelela khon' akukhon' okungasiphilisa
Isikhathi sethu sehlukile kwesenu,

Ngezikhathi zenu nanifuy' ochibidolo;
Namuhl' abelusi basezikolweni.
Nina nanibuk' omakhelwane ngokwemizi;
Thina sibabuka ngokwamazwe omhlaba.
Eleth' ikusasa liqhazile kunelenu

BUKELANI MMELLY SHANGASE

GENERATIONS

The great-grandparents complained about grandfather.
Grandfather complained about father;
Father complains about me.
Father says a child does not talk back to him
His word is final and should be followed.
But where did it start to go wrong, generationally?
Each generation blames the one which comes next?
What must be fixed so that things are set right?

I see a future that is bright;
Those rearing me up say, they are not sure, they are
 sceptical.
What I do those that are rearing me up do not like
They say they did not do things the way I do.
They say they respected their own parents.
They say I do not respect them.
They say I am looking for reasons for what they say.
They say I listen to friends too much.

But who must I listen to?
But to whom is my future dependent on?
But who knows about my future?
Those rearing me up know about yesterday;
Those rearing me up do not know about tomorrow;
Things of yesterday are not similar to that of tomorrow
But who should know what is to be done
So that tomorrow is anticipated?

Parents set us free so that we see for ourselves;
What you have planned for us is not what can make us

live.
Our time is different from your time,
In your time you kept livestock aplenty;
Today the herders are at school.
You looked at neighbours in terms of nearby surrounding houses;
We look at neighbours in terms of countries of the world.
Our future is brighter than yours

Translated from the Zulu original – Bukelani Mmelly Shangase's Izizukulwane – by Dr Innocentia Jabulisile Mhlambi

INDULI YEXHWAYELO

IsiXhosa

Induli yaseMarikana; induli yexhwayelo
Apho kwahl'inyhikityha yokufa kwabembi zimbiwa
Bezomba phants' emathunjini omhlaba.

Imizimba yamaxhoba neengxwelerha;
yantyumpantyumpeka kwebomvu imbola
isezela elembol' ebomvu ivumba.

Imizimba izimbobo ngembobo zimbumbulu
zitaka kwintunjana, kwintanda yezandla zamaPolisa
kaRhulumente wentando yesininzi.

Unobangela ziintshukumo zezikhalazo
Kukhalazelwa unyuselo mvuzo ngabasebenzi
Loo ntshukumo yamitha yazala: Iingxwelerha,
    abahlolokazi,
Iinkedama, imiz' engenamadoda, abantwan' abaswel'
    oYise,
Kunye neentsaph' eziswel' abondli.

Funqu! umthamo kwizibhedlela ngenxa yeengxwelerha
Yakukuxakeka kubongi, abongikazi nooGqirha;
Kusindiswa ubomi bezo ngxwelerha,
Zimbi ziqatyulwa kwingqaqambo ezimandla
Zimbi zaphulukana nobomi kwintaba yexhwayelo.

Yaba lukrozo lwezithuthi;
zijonga ngomva amakhaya ngokwentsebenzo
zijongise amabombo kwawokuzalwa amakhaya
Ezinye zisinda-sindeka zizidumbu

Zimbi zisinda-sindeka ngabembi mgodi
benxunguphele emphefumlweni, besopha iintliziyo
bambi bentliziyo zinamahlwili kukuthinjelwa oogxa babo
kukufa.

Emakhaya; yanda imihlambi yamangcwaba.
Noxa sele amila ingca loo mangcwaba nje!
Kwiintsapho ezohlulwe nezihlobo zazo
oku kosana olulele lulila isingqala asinasiqabu.

        SIWAPHIWE FORTUNE SHWENI

THE HILL OF AGONY

The Marikana Hill of agony,
Where miners died brutally.
They had to work underground.
Bodies of victims and casualties,
Died in pools of the so-called ochre.

While miners were sniffing blood,
Their bodies had bullet holes.
Bullets were from the Police hands.
Police of our Democratic Government.
Miners were complaining, that's the cause!

Armed miners decided to demonstrate and protest,
Demanded living wages and increase from their employers.
Miners' deaths, poor widows, appalled citizens!
Fatherless orphans, hunger, struggling families,
Those were the Marikana Hill consequences!

The Health civil servants moved up and down,
Did their best to save casualties, but we lost others.
From gunshots other miners died instantly.
Sprawled bodies filled the Marikana Hill.
The unforgettable scene of agony!

Affected families had to transport bodies,
From Marikana to the homes of the deceased.
Heartbroken citizens buried their breadwinners,
While other miners returned being disabled.
The sting of death caused so much pain!

Cemeteries had additional unexpected graves!
Heads of families were butchered ruthlessly.
Their families were left groaning with pain.
Graves without tombstones are covered with grass.
But the martyrs underground cannot be forgotten!

Translated from the Xhosa original – Siwaphiwe Fortune Shweni's Induli Yexhwayelo – by Angelinah Dazela

ANINA

ENGLISH

[1]I enjoyed the feeling
of rubbing my body against
anything I could
the thick lip of the bathtub
with no one in the house
cupboard doors
corner of beds sometimes
my hands

I wanted to rub myself against
something moving
so I brought one boy
home from school
It wasn't the first time
All the boys knew

That woman came home
from work early and
I was on top of him
he pushed me off
covered himself ran out
saying, Sorry, Auntie! Sorry!
I couldn't help but laugh

She caught me, dragged me
to the stove screaming
and switching both plates on
Her length of beautiful hair
swung close enough for me
to pull if my hands weren't

on the plates, my palms sizzled

Later she told me
I was disgusting
I was a filthy girl
No wonder you killed your mother
Then she came to me with
the butter for my hands

[2]I heard parts of what she said to my father,
I don't know what's wrong with that girl…
you must punish her for this…
she must calm down now…
you must take her out from school…
she's a filthy, ungrateful child…
she must get a job in a factory…
what will the neighbours say?
I only heard my father say,
When she was small,
I always found her with her hand down there

FRANCINE SIMON

DEEPA

ENGLISH

Neela, I come down on you
                                    your legs separate mine
you tell me you are good at waiting
                                my hips give way to your tongue
reaches in my mouth of ancestors
                                the mouth of cousin-sisters
your hand comes around my trunk
                                cut the first lips of my gurhal

Neela, you bend my skull	lick up my kantha here
	Please!
I will lick yours	you tell me
I must say if I don't want	what you ask me to do
our vulvae bear and bear	and bear until
jalebi wet	we must leave this
	crematorium
for feast	to wait

                                         FRANCINE SIMON

NTWA YA BANA BA THARI

SETSWANA

Bana ba motho baalwana
Ba jana ka dinatha magobe
Bana ba kgwale ba tlhoka go bitsana ka melodi
Ke mpelegolole ke go lae
Ya re botlhogo putswa ba bua ba re
Ka tlhagolela mooka
Ya re o gola wa ntlhaba

Bontsi bo shebile dimpa
Ba lelwa ditilo go ja ka dimpa tse pedi
E re ditletse ba tlatse marama
Fa lemme le le mo bojeleng
Ba tlhoke go lekgaoganya
Jaaka tlhogo ya tsie
Yo monnye le yo mogolo
Ba tlhoke letswalo
Mme ba bolaye yo mongwe ntlheng ya bogagapa
Go tsaya lemme ele go ikhumisa
Ntswa khumo le lehuma di lala mmogo

Bana ba motho ba lwana
Moopedi fa a opela a re
Tlogela bana ba motho ba lwane
Bangwe ba tle batimi batlhoki tshono
Mme batlhoki ba tlhokele ruri

Ka khumo ele segwagwa e pharuma
E re e pharumile o ba tshwantse
Ba polotika fa go batliwa ditshwanelo tsa botho
Ba bua polotiki
Balwani ba ditshwanelo ba fetoge mapantiti

                        TIISETSO THIBA

CIVIL WAR

Siblings are fighting
Tearing at each other
Children of same parents, blood should be thicker than
    water
Let me tell you something
Seek wisdom from old generations
Keeping a snake warm didn't mean it wouldn't bite me

Many care only about their stomachs
It's an immense fight for hierarchy
More pockets are filling up
While you continue to drink to stupor
They divide and conquer
Old and new all the same
Have no fear no doubt
It's survival of the fittest
The weak must be eliminated
While the rich get richer

Brethren is fighting
When the singer sings and says
Let them fight it out
They must deny the poor a chance
And the poor remain destitute
While the rich reign supreme

The supremist will only come to enemy lines
To stand in the way of human rights endeavour
Talking politics
The freedom fighters are now prisoners

Translated from the Setswana original – Tiisetso Thiba's Ntwa Ya Bana Ba Thari – by Goodenough Mashego

FREEDOM

ENGLISH

leaves a window open
lifts the latch
lets itself out

Freedom travels across boundaries
passes dark hours, rides the tall wave
feels the furnace

Freedom pushes and struggles
cries and sheds blood
arrives different – new

Freedom waits, active and still
undoes and unwinds
looks behind and beyond

Freedom powers its own house
reaches and
holds unknown music

Freedom unfreezes its streams
looks afresh
at the face of another

Freedom broods, gives birth
in the blood of itself
is never alone

				ELIZABETH TREW

LIKE SILHOUETTES (AFTER FATHERLESS KIDS)

ENGLISH

Silhouettes: the ever-present not so real people.
Always there
but not really even there.
That is what it is like to have a father
who was there
but not really even there; a silhouette.

When your father is a silhouette
you learn to embrace memories tightly until you suck the past out their bones

When your father is a silhouette
your mother masters the art of Sciography,
carefully constructing silhouettes that portray your father as a work of art,
leaving you to fill in the featureless voids of the skeleton

When your father is a silhouette
you learn that not all shadows belong to bodies
nor all bodies belong to their silhouettes

When your father is a silhouette
you ravage through the remnants of his footprints and shadow
keeping every bit and piece of his existence tucked under

   your pillow
hoping that when you wake up
the tooth fairy will have swapped the silhouette for the
   real thing

THATO TSHUKUDU

INNOCENT

AFRIKAANS

Sy toets haar oksels:
sy het nog haar slaaphemp aan
al het sy vroeg ver gestap.

Innocent sweet oor die pik:
hy grawe 'n fondasie
vir die raised gardens vir haar PermaCulture.

Sy sit op die stoep agter haar laptop,
maak vir hom tee,
herinner hom dat hy vloeistof moet inkry,

vir die son
(hy drink dit soet).

Die son vat lank om bo te kom.
Dit bly voormiddag.

Hy hou van sy spiere
waarvoor hy geoefen het:
'n ysterpaal
met twee sement gewigte
in 3-liter verfblikke gevorm.

Sy dink
hy droom oor Johannesburg
terwyl hy bou en grawe en bosse uitkap.

Iets byt haar –
sy is geskok

oor die wit vet wat bokant die denim hang
waar sy die bosluis aftrek.

Dit bly jeuk
die hele warm dag.

     ELNA VAN NIEKERK

INNOCENT

She checks her armpits:
she's still wearing her pyjama top
despite going for a long, early stroll.

Innocent sweats over the pick:
he's digging a foundation
for the raised gardens for her PermaCulture.

She sits on the stoep behind her laptop,
makes him some tea
reminds him to take enough fluids,

for the sun
(he drinks it sweet).

The sun takes its time to rise.
It remains morning.

He likes his muscles
for which he trained:
an iron pole
with two cement weights
formed in 3-litre paint cans.

She thinks
he's dreaming about Johannesburg
while he's building and digging and felling bushes.

Something bites her –
she's shocked

by the white fat hanging over the denim
where she removes the tick.

It keeps on itching
the whole hot day.

Translated from the Afrikaans original – Elna van Niekerk's
Innocent – by Pieter Odendaal

BELHAR

AFRIKAANS

ek is saam met die mense van Belhar
by 'n stakeholder feedback session
van die Safe Choices 4 Youth projek

sulke goed begin laat

uiteindelik het ek ook klaar gepraat
maar hulle vra my om die vote of thanks te doen
heel aan die einde
so ek moet nog konsentreer

voor die tyd het ek twee witmense gevra
waar is Bellville South se gemeenskapsaal:
hulle het my verkeerd verduidelik
en die Garmin het ook nie geweet nie

langs my sit 'n tannie:
sy's netjies aangetrek maar sy lyk bietjie verward
soos my ma
as sy nie mooi hoor wat gebeur nie

ek wonder wie vanoggend haar oorbelletjies ingehaak het

die International Funders
weet nie presies wat hulle will sien nie,
sit met beton smiles
en kyk na die rou talent
van die teenagers van Belhar:
gerapte boodskappe in gemengde Afrikaans
(vir hulle verlore)

agter die handjies
wat kruis oor die kruis
en amper dáár vat

jy wonder wat hulle dink maar gee vandag nie om nie

jy is deel daarvan

dis warm en mense stem nie saam nie
en mense wat jy uitgenooi het kom nie
en ander wat jy gehoop het
kom nie
is nou daar
en iemand het nie die brief verstaan nie
en nie alles vloei inmekaar nie

nie alles werk mooi uit nie

die program herkonstrueer rondom die wat daar is
(in plaas van die MEC en die burgemeester
het ons die CPF en die Neighbourhoodwatch)

Dan the Floor Killer vat die vloer

nou en dan kyk die tannie na my vir 'n cue
oor hoe sy moet reageer
maar ek is 'n gas
en ek is wit

en sy is nie seker of my gedrag
wel appropriate to the occasion is nie
die drama kinders skree in die mikrofoon
en dit laat die ou mense verbouereerd rondkyk:
wat gebeur nou?
hulle lag saam
sonder dat hulle verstaan

na middagete
wat genoeg is en betyds

(met die soort events weet mens nie altyd nie)

verlaat 'n paar mense die saal.

die tannie wat my aan my ma laat dink
groet my met 'n drukkie en sê
sy's bly ons het ontmoet,

sy gaan nou huis toe loop.

ELNA VAN NIEKERK

BELHAR

I'm joining the people of Belhar
at a stakeholder feedback session
for the Safe Choices 4 Youth project

these things start late

eventually I'm also done talking
but they ask me to do the vote of thanks
right at the end
so I still need to concentrate

beforehand I asked two white people
where Bellville South's community hall was;
they misdirected me
and the Garmin also didn't know

a lady is seated next to me:
she's neatly dressed but looks a bit perplexed
like my mom
when she can't quite hear what's going on

I wonder who put in her earrings today

the International Funders
don't exactly know what they want to see,
they sit with concrete smiles
and stare at the raw talent
of Belhar's teenagers:
rapped messages in mixed Afrikaans
(lost to them)

behind the hands
that cross the cross
and almost meet there

you wonder what they're thinking but you don't care
 today

you are part of it

it's hot and the people are disagreeing
and people that you invited didn't pitch
and others who you hoped
wouldn't come
are there now
and someone didn't understand the brief
and not everything is flowing smoothly

not everything is working out

the programme reconstructs around those who are there
(instead of the MEC and mayor
we have the CPF and the Neighbourhood watch)

Dan the Floor Killer takes to the floor

now and then the lady looks at me for a cue
as to how she should react
but I am a guest
and I am white
and she doesn't know if my behaviour

is in fact appropriate to the occasion

the drama kids shout into the microphone
the older people look around flustered:
what's happening now?
they laugh along
without understanding

after lunch
which is enough and on time
(with these kinds of events one doesn't always know)
a few people leave the hall.

that lady who reminds me of my mother
greets me with a hug and says
she's glad we met,

she's walking home now.

*Translated from the Afrikaans original – Elna van Niekerk's Belhar
– by Pieter Odendaal*

DIE OVERALL VAN MY

AFRIKAANS

'k staan op
vat 'n skoon hemp
uit die kas.
Trek hom aan ma
hy passie so lekker nie:
die collar is te styf
die moue te lank.

Gan Woolworths
toe vir hulle vaal, netjiese skool
broeke ma
dis te styf hie ommie hol;
vir kort bene
issie pype te lank.

Huur 'n suit vir my Matriek-afskeid,
so 'n blinke soos 'n krismislint.
Mos die blinkste is die stylish-ste.
Behalwe dis te styf hie ommie hol
te nou hie
en te wyd daa.

Wêk in 'n kantoor daa innie Kaap.
Stres oorrie regte skoene
en huil amper
wannie donnerse klere in allie donnerse winkels passie.
Viloorrie job ôk
wat fine is.

Kry 'n paint job op die plaas
lê lank leeg by die huis
– Willie Werker –
en Pa was ook 'n painter.
Die mense wonne sieke al lank al
wanneer my hoogmoed gan val
en ek in Pa se voetspore sal volg.

'k sit af Ko-Op
toe en krap deur die rakke
vir 'n wit overall
en pas hom an.
Die donnerse ding sit toe reg
hie ommie hol, ommie bene,
alles.
Die donnerse ding pas my
soos 'n handskoen.

    LESTER WALBRUGH

THIS OVERALL OF MINE

I get up
take a clean shirt
from the closet.
Put it on but
it doesn't quite fit:
the collar is too tight
the sleeves too long.

Off to Woolworths
for their grey, neat school
pants but
they're too tight here around the ass;
the legs are too long
for short limbs.

Hire a suit for my Matric farewell,
shiny like a Christmas ribbon.
The shinier, the fleeker, right?
Except it's too tight here around the ass
too narrow here
and too wide there.

Work in an office there in the Cape.
Stress about the right shoes
and almost cry
'coz the bloody clothes in all the bloody stores don't fit
Lose the job too
which is fine.

Get a paint job on the farm
Been idling my time away at home
– Willie Werker –
and Dad was a painter too.
People have probably been wondering
when my pride would come to a fall
and I would follow in Dad's footsteps.

I'm off to Co-Op
and rummage through the shelves
for a white overall
and try it on.
The bloody thing hugs me just fine
here around the ass, around the legs,
everything.
The bloody thing fits me
like a glove.

Translated from the Afrikaans original – Lester Walbrugh's Die Overall Van My – by Pieter Odendaal

CITY DUMP

ENGLISH

The cold nights are coming in
and those who have no home
other than the municipal dump,
are lighting fires in paint tins
to fall asleep in the tiny warmth.

When it jumps to brush and grass
the town wakes to acrid smoke,
hanging like guilt in the air.

JEANNIE WALLACE MCKEOWN

ACCUMULATED GRIEF

ENGLISH

In the four months
since my mother died
I have been to five funerals.

At each one I mourn
more than the person
whose name
is on the leaflet.

    CRYSTAL WARREN

DETAILS OF DEATH

At the dentist
for the first time
after your funeral
I realise
I need to change
the next of kin.

Crossing out your name
would be hard enough,
but the records are in pencil
and I am handed a rubber
to erase you from my file,
from my life.

    CRYSTAL WARREN

STATE OF THE NATION

ENGLISH

I go to the pharmacy
to fill my prescription,
collect another month
of my chronic medication.

They tell me they are out of stock
of two of the tablets.
They can help my cholesterol
but the high blood pressure tablets
and antidepressants
are sold out.

They give me a few tablets
to tide me over,
from a precious store
sourced from other
chemists in town,
who are also low on supplies.
They promise to deliver
as soon as the new stock arrives.

I am not sure
if I should be relieved
that I am not alone
in my affliction,
or concerned

that so many people
in this small city
are also
stressed and depressed.

CRYSTAL WARREN

IMMIGRANT

ENGLISH

salty breezes call to my senses.
I awake to the Spanish sun
teasing the horizon, the
ocean giggles and glistens.

fruits and cheese and wine
lay spread for morning feasts;
the pavements singing
sizzling songs of decadence.

matadors parade their crisp attire
as we stroll through the cobled square.
a bandurria's melody recalls
an elderly couple's youthful love.

and the creeking door of my tin shack
reminds me, home remains a memory.

FLOW WELLINGTON

APOLLONIAN TRICK

ENGLISH

The sombre display draws a crowd to the square –
a shuffle of ashen young men clothed in chains
red-brown with time, heavy with memory. In turn

they shed their dress onto a mountainous pile, coiled,
hissing in the low sun. With shining faces the men
skip away in white rags and Phrygian caps. But

as soon as they leave, their shackles grow back.
The puzzled crowd thins as one last man appears, too
shuffling under metal restraints. He labours to cast

his demons to the tangled beast. Unlike those before,
he struts away, forever without chains, having traded
white rag and cap, for black robe and mortarboard.

ATHOL WILLIAMS

BIOGRAPHIES

Zukiswa Muriel Adonis is a 42-year-old food technologist who loves arts and culture, i.e. listening to and reading poetry (Xhosa and English), reading Xhosa and English novels, watching drama/theatre performances (Xhosa, English and a bit of Afrikaans). Baxter and Artscape are her second homes. She loves travelling (locally and internationally) and visiting museums (for their sculptures and photographs). She enjoys window shopping for clothes and ornaments in flea markets and writes Xhosa poems as a hobby.

Jim Pascual Agustin was born in Marikina, the shoemaking industry capital of the Philippines. He lives on the fringes of Cape Town with his lovely wife and twin daughters, along with an ageing dog and a stray cat that decided to stay. He has published poetry collections in Filipino and English since 1992. His work has appeared in *Rhino, World Literature Today, Modern Poetry in Translation, New Coin, Aerodrome and New Contrast among others.* His latest poetry collection, *How to Make a Salagubang Helicopter*, is due to be released by San Anselmo Publications in 2018. Agustin also writes a blog (www.matangmanok.wordpress.com).

Du Toit Albertze is a theatre-maker, scriptwriter and poet. He is currently working on his BA honours degree in theatre directing at Stellenbosch University. Some of his theatre work includes: *Bos*, *Vaselinetjie*, *Die Reëngodin*, *Kommapunt*, *Steriel*, *(W)asem* and *Die Meermin Kompleks*. As a spoken word poet he has been part of the Inzync Poetry Collection team for more than three years. He is an artist who strongly supports queer, feminist and mental health issues and believes strongly in the breaking down of destructive Afrikaner structures.

Kyle Allan is a writer, recording artist and event organiser. He has published two books of poetry, *House without walls* (2016) and *The space between us* (2018), and has released one album, *Influences* (2013).

Mia Arderne is a writer, columnist and poet from Cape Town. She performed at the McGregor Poetry Festival in 2017 and was published in the *Sol Plaatje European Union Poetry Anthology* in 2013. She completed her MA in English creative writing at UCT after receiving the NRF Freestanding Masters scholarship. Her columns have been published by *Marie Claire*, *City Press*, *GQ* magazine and *Matador Network* among others. Her short stories have appeared in various anthologies and her debut novel was short-listed for the Dinaane Debut Fiction Award. Her writing explores themes of identity, marginalisation and sexuality.

Vonani Bila is the author of five books of poems in English and eight storybooks for newly literate adult readers in Xitsonga, Sepedi and English. Bila is a driving force in South African poetry as the founding editor of the *Timbila* poetry journal, publisher of Timbila books and founder of Timbila Writers' Village, a rural retreat centre for writers. He teaches in the Department of English Studies at the University of Limpopo.

René Bohnen is an Afrikaans poet who was born and bred in KZN. She now lives in Johannesburg and in the Western Cape, working as a freelance writer, translator and photographer. She holds a master's degree in Creative

Writing and has published three books of poetry, *Spoorsny* (2000), *in die niks al om* (2011) and *Op die vingerpunte van die heelal* (2017).

Christine Coates is a poet and writer from Cape Town. She has an MA in creative writing from the University of Cape Town. Her poems and stories have been published in various literary journals. Her debut collection, *Homegrown*, published in 2014 by Modjaji Books, received an honourable mention from the Glenna Luschei Prize. Her second collection will be published later in 2018. Her poems have been selected for the *Sol Plaatje European Union Poetry* anthologies every year since inception: 2011–2017, and *Best "New" African Poets* 2015 and 2016 anthologies.

Silulundi Coki ngumfundi owenza unyaka wesithathu kwiDyunisithi yaseKapa (University of Cape Town). Uyaluthanda ulwimi de esikolweni ufunda Isixhosa, Isingesi kunye neSociology. Uzibona engumbhali owaziwa jikelele, ebhala ngelwimi lenkobe isiXhosa kutsho. Masibuyeleni embo.

Mark de Wet is a published author living in KZN. He is hoping to publish two books this year, one of which is a 'visual fusion of wine and poetry' and is 150 verses long, based on the *Rubaiyat of Omar Khayham*, written a thousand years ago. Poetry has always been one of his 'secret loves'.

Luthando Dlamini was born in Margate, KwaZulu-Natal. He is an LLB student at the University of Cape Town.

Ruth Everson is a poet, writer and speaker who uses her

work to encourage, inspire and inquire. She has presented lectures and workshops on poetry and creativity at festivals, schools, conferences and gatherings across South Africa. Her poetry has taken her to China, Egypt, Lesotho, Swaziland and Botswana. For her, to quote one of her poems: "Poetry is dangerous, Poetry will write your tears in ink, Poetry will hang your soul on barbed wire lines."

Nobuntu Gantana is a lover of all forms of art. Her fascination with languages is what fuelled her passion in writing. She is currently based in Grahamstown where she is studying part-time and working as a government official. In her personal capacity she mentors young girls on life-skills. Her writing explores various social issues affecting women in society. One of her poems was published in Volume VI of the *Sol Plaatje European Union Poetry Anthology* in 2016. Her second poem 'Dadobawo ndicel' amandla' was published in Volume VII of the same poetry anthology in 2017.

Sarah Godsell was born in 1985, in Johannesburg, South Africa. She is a historian and poet. She began performing in 2009 and has performed nationally and internationally on various stages, radio and TV platforms. She has been published in journals such as *Poetry Potion*, *New Coin*, *Astra* and *Illuminations*, and her words appear in edited collections such as *Home is Where the Mic is* and *Marikana: A Moment in Time*. Her first collection, *Seaweed Sky*, came out in 2016, and was a finalist for the HSS Fiction Awards in 2018.

Richard Higgs is a lecturer in digital curation at the University of Cape Town. He holds master's degrees in language sciences and creative writing. He was born in

Boksburg and is a keen amateur actor and director, as well as an activist for autism.

Veronique Jephtas is a 21-year-old final-year drama and theatre studies student at Stellenbosch University. She is specialising in directing and voice art. Jephtas is a firm believer in the fact that she cannot do everything, but what she can do she can do very good. Her goal is to be a storyteller. She wants and loves to go to places in her stories where others are too scared to go. Her passion lies in performing and writing. She always strives to not only learn, but to learn to apply, to listen, to be.

Zandile Khumalo is a 31-year-old new writer, born and bred in Mariannhill outside of Durban. Molle is an aspiring novelist who is currently working on her debut fantasy/adventure novel. Her poem 'Ngenze Nami Ngizigqaje' is a young girl's yearning for a soulmate.

Thabiso Tsietsi Lakajoe ke mongodi wa dithothokiso Sesotho. Lakajoe ke mongodi ya lwanelang setso le ditokelo tsa puo ya letswele hore le yona e tshwane e hlokomelwe jwaloka puo tse ding. Tse ding tsa dithothokiso tsa hae di phatlaladitswe ho *ITCH* journal, *Poetry Potion*, AvBob Poetry Competition, *Love Letters to My Child*, 2015, 2016 & 2017 *Sol Plaatjie European Union Poetry Anthology*.

George Thabiso Leseba is a University of the Free State student, poet, writer and motivator. He is very passionate about mother tongue and is not afraid to express his feelings through it. He is a winner of the regional Ubuntu competitions for kids' radio, and he represented QwaQwa Radio on a national level with his Sotho essay that came in second place and left many people craving more.

Busisiwe Mahlangu is a writer, perfomer and TEDx speaker. She is the founder of Lwazilubanzi, a community-based project aimed at using literature as a tool of resistance and healing. She has performed her work around South Africa, including Open Book Festival (CPT), Words In My Mouth Slam Week (Mpumalanga) and the Vavasati International Women's Festival. Her poetry was longlisted for the Sol Plaatje European Union Poetry Award in 2017.

Tshepiso Makgoloane is a 21-year-old visionary who was raised in a village called Patantshwane at Sekhukhune district. She later moved to Motetema where she currently resides. She has aspired to write in both Sepedi and English since 2014 when she was still in high school and she is currently a committed LLB student at the University of South Africa.

Mbali Malimela is a strictly isiZulu female writer and perfomer from KZN. She has showcased some of her work on the national radio station UKhozi.fm. She has also perfomed on different stages around Durban, like The Bat Centre, Playhouse Theatre (Sundowners) and the Durban Poetry Show (DPS), as well as in Cape Town, at the Baxter Theatre & Obviouzly Armchair.

Anga Mamfanya is a spoken word artist based in Pretoria. He made his performance debut in 2016 at the Tshwane Speak Out Loud Youth Poetry Competition, in which he was the 2nd prize winner. He has shared his original work at the University of Johannesburg and the University of Pretoria as a guest speaker. Mamfanya is the founder of

Blvcksuburbia, a social movement that aims to empower black communities through poetry and art.

Sibulelo Manamatela is a literature student and poet based in Johannesburg. She is a great lover of any worthwhile written text whether it is in novels, plays, music or poetry. Perhaps it is language that she is really in love with.

Tshedza Mashamba is a 17-year-old South African black female currently doing her matric year at Hyde Park High School. She began writing in 2015 and is a published author of three poems and one short story.

Bongani Masilela is a native of South Africa born in 1992. He is a mathematician, poet and a human rights activist who was born with a physical disability. Masilela has authored a poetry anthology titled *Then I don't want to be a Poet*. Despite him having studied mathematics, his love for art and sport is massive.

Aaron Mpho Masowa is an author and analyst of Sesotho books, and a teacher. He has currently published four books. Namely *Jo, bophelo bona!*, *Lenyora* and *Dikakata tsa bophel*. He is currently pursuing a PhD with the University of the Free State.

Zongezile Matshoba can be found wherever there is a literary event for the young and old. His writings narrate the humour and hardships of township and rural life and interrogate whether it is yet uhuru in people's livelihood.

Katise Mawela is a Johannesburg-based award-winning poet and cultural activist. His poems have appeared in various publications including *Tribute* magazine. He is also a freelance journalist.

Marthe McLoud is 'n maatskaplike werker en woon in die Strand. Verskeie van haar gedigte en kortverhale is op Litnet gepubliseer. In 2017 was sy een van die *Nuwe Stemme 6* wat deur Tafelberg uitgegee is, waarin ses van haar gedigte gepubliseer is. Van haar gedigte het ook in 2018 in die *New Contast Literary Journal* verskyn.

Janine Milne holds a bachelor's degree in theory of literature and creative writing, with distinctions, from the University of South Africa. She won the McGregor Poetry Festival poetry competition and had several poems published in *The Sol Plaatje European Union Poetry Anthology* Volume IV. Her short stories were chosen for the coveted *Short Sharp Stories Anthology*, *Die Laughing* and *The Bloody Parchment*, the 2016 South African Horror Festival anthology. She is currently working on her first poetry collection and novel.

Thabiso Mofokeng started writing at the age of 15. He is a versatile writer – writing in Sesotho and English. Some of his Sesotho books are prescribed by the Department of Education for Grade 8 and Grade 10. After working as a self-made Sesotho language practitioner, he found himself becoming the founding publisher of Mosa Media and Book Distributors (Pty) Ltd – excelling in publishing books written in African languages. Thabiso completed his Master of Arts in creative writing with distinctions at Rhodes University in 2015. He is currently studying a PhD in English at the University of the Western Cape. He is a 2016/17 Dinaane Debut Fiction Award Finalist. He was named as one of the *Mail and Guardian* #200 Young South Africans 2017. His latest novel is *The Last Stop*.

Daniel Matsepe Mohlala is a 27-year-old BCom graduate (University of Limpopo) from the rural village of Moeding, on the outskirts of Marble Hall. A poet who aspires to write in Sepedi, his love for literature began when he was in high school. In April 2018 he co-authored a book titled *Broken Dreams: The Awakening Past* with Edwin D Mabodimo Mphaga. He previously served as a freelance translator for *Sekhukhune Times* newspaper. He currently lives in Motetema. He has a daughter named Bohlale.

Dikeledi Mokoena is a black woman born in Sebokeng, a township in South Africa. She is a PhD candidate in political science and lectures African feminism and gender studies at the Thabo Mbeki African Leadership Institute. She identifies with some 'isms' such as pan-Africanism and African feminism. She is a lover of laughter and life and reveres God and her ancestors.

Mjele Msimang is a Tshwane-based poet, fiction writer and educator. He began writing in 2016 as a way of self-exploration and self-awareness. His work is highly influenced by rap, hiphop and history. He has guest lectured history through poetry at the universities of the Witwatersrand and Johannesburg and has performed on various stages in and around Johannesburg and Tshwane. His poems seek to explore himself and his surroundings, speaking to structural inequality, personal triumphs and loss, family, love, sexuality, culture and traditions. He hopes that through his writing he can add to the voices battling for a brighter, more inclusive future and history.

Moses Mtileni is the author of *Mpimavayeni* (a novel), *Nhlalala* (a novel) and *U Ya Va Rungula* (poetry). He has curated a Xitsonga poetry anthology, *Ntsena loko Mpfula A Yo Sewula*, and has translated the works of, among others, Peter Horn and Ngũgĩ wa Thiong'o into Xitsonga. His poetry has appeared in a few volumes of the *Sol Plaatje European Union Poetry Anthology*, *Illuminations*, *Asymptote*, *Timbila*, *Botsotso*, and *Poetry Potion*. He comes from Nkuri-Tomu Village in Limpopo.

Sifiso Mtshali was raised and educated in Daveyton. He is an aspiring poet and an upcoming writer. He has been shortlisted twice in the SA Writers College short story competition. Mtshali is passionate about all things classical, from paintings to literature, he is a lover of words and the power they wield.

Sinaso Mxakaza is a young South African writer who started writing in 2008 inspired by her love for books. Her poems are about healing, change and finding one's voice in the world we live in. Her work has been published online on sites such as VoicesNet, Fundza and in online anthologies like *Poetry Potion* and *Next Generation Speaks Global Youth Anthology*.

Pamela Newham is a journalist, author of children's books and a poet. She runs workshops on journalism and writing books for children. She lives in Cape Town. Her poems have been published in anthologies and literary journals. Her poetry collection, *Washing Day in the Bush*, was published in 2017.

Sandile Ngidi is a poet, translator, freelance journalist and dramatist. He was born in Vryheid in 1969 and grew up in Amahlongwa on the south coast of Durban. He is the Zulu-to-English translator of Sibusiso Nyembezi's classic Zulu novel, *Inkinsela yaseMgungundlovu*. He is currently an MA creative writing student at Rhodes University.

Bomikazi Njoloza is a versatile writer, poet and advocate for mother-tongue literacy; a child and student of the universe. She arrived on this planet over two decades ago in the land of silent hills, iminga and scarlet aloes. This daughter of forgiveness moulds poetry; speaks and tells stories in more ways than we have found a language for. As Zakes Mda said in a foreword to her debut anthology, 'hers is a voice that demands to be heard'. Njoloza's debut poetry anthology, *The Colour of Love*, was published in 2012 and she has since published extensively in isiXhosa, English and German.

Simphiwe Nolutshungu is a published poet and writer. Last year he won a SALA award in poetry. He holds a master's degree in creative writing and is a teacher by qualification. He works as a lecturer at the University of Cape Town, in the Department of African Languages and Literature, and is currently pursuing his PhD in IsiXhosa.

Zola Nongogo was born in the Eastern Cape in Mount Ayliff and currently lives in Cape Town. He has been published in *Prufrock* magazine, *The Sol Plaatje European Union Poetry Anthology* in 2015 and 2017 and the online literary journal *Eunoia Review* under the name Zukisani Nongogo.

USipho Albert Ntombela wazalelwa eMnambithi

eMatiwaneskop kwesenkosi uShabalala nokuyilapha afunda khona imfundo yamabanga aphansi.Waqala ukufunda eCwembe BC School wase edlulela eMangcengeza Secondary School wagcina ephothule ibanga leshumi Emhlwaneni High School. Waqhubeka wafundela ubuthisha eBethel College of Education kusuka ngonyaka we-1988 kuya kowe-1990. Ngonyaka we-1991 waqala ukufundisa eQhudeni Public School eNkandla. Ezinye izikole aseke wafundisa kuzo UMgazi Public School, Lerato-uThando High School kanye Heritage Combined School. Useke waba yiNhloko yeziLimi ezikolweni ezehlukene, ibamba likaThishanhloko, uThisha-nhloko kanye noMeluleki wezikolo olimini lwesiZulu. Ngesikhathi efundisa ubefunda ngasese e-Unisa waze waphothula iziqu zobudokotela. Ngonyaka we-2012 waqala ukufundisa eWits School of Education nokuyilapho enguMphathi welimi zabampisholo.

Mushayathoni Bridget Nwovhe is a medical student and the author of a book titled *Calendar's Time*. She's also an editor at her recently found publishing company (Yoanda Khano Publishing), a speaker and a mentor to many. She has been featured in many different newspapers, like *Limpopo Mirror*, and has been interviewed on radio stations like Phalaphala FM. She believes in healing through poetry and medicine, which is maybe why she's doing both.

Hans Pienaar has published two collections of poetry (*Die Taal van Voëls*, *Notas uit die Empire*) in Afrikaans and one of photo-poems (*Uithoeke/Outcorners*). He is a former chair of the Melville Poetry Festival. He has also written three works of fiction and written and produced several plays. He won the Pansa national award for *Three Dozen Roses*, the Marius Jooste Prize for his MA in creative writing (cum laude), the Rapport Prize for Non-Fiction and the Cosaw Prize for short stories. His poems and stories have been anthologised in various collections.

Sehloho Piet Rampai was born in 1985 and has a law degree from NMMU. He has published regularly with *Poetry Potion*.

Juliette Rose-Innes is a 19-year-old Capetonian living in Woodstock. She was a finalist for the Scribe Scriptwriting Competition (2017) and has been published in *English Alive* (2016 and 2017). She currently attends the University of Cape Town and is studying a degree in theatre and performance, aspiring to write and direct plays. Her favourite writers include Kurt Vonnegut, John Irving, Samuel Beckett and Emily Berry. Along with writing, she enjoys reading, photography and wearing unfashionable clothes.

Deborah Seddon is a poet, feminist and academic. She was born and raised in Harare, Zimbabwe. She has lived and worked in Grahamstown, in the Eastern Cape, for a long time. She teaches poetry, Early Modern Literature, African-American, African, and Afro-Caribbean literature at USKAR, the University Still Known as Rhodes. Her current research focuses on South African and African-American spoken word, and on queer literature and film.

Moses Seletisha is a radical performance poet, translator and author of *Tšhutšhumakgala* (his first published title). He is a native writer who hails from the deep rural areas of Ga-Matlala 'a Rakgwadi (Tsimanyane village), not far from Marble Hall in the then Northern Province. An intellectual whose area of interest is African languages and their social context, Seletisha has chosen to restrict himself from writing in any language other than Sepedi. By any means necessary, Seletisha prides himself as having been circumcised by notable Sepedi writers such as Goodenough Mashego, Dr David Maahlamela, Matete Motsoaledi and more not mentioned. Some of his work has been featured in various forms of literary journals, that include the *Botsotso* poetry anthology and *megaArtists* magazine. He is the winner of the Sol Plaatje European Union Poetry Award 2017 and the winner of the South African Literary Award as First-time Published Author (2017). He was invited by the National Library of South Africa to perform a poem "Kgadime" – in celebration of OK Matsepe. Pula!

Nkwana Joshua Serutle is a writer, spoken word poet and fine artist, who was born and raised outside Burgersfort, Limpopo. In 2017 he joined Mzansi Poetry Academy to enhance his writing skills. His work draws much attention on the streets, shifting paradigms on social issues. Some of his highlights in 2017 included performing on SABC 1's, YoTV. Later on that year he became Top 10 finalist for Leleme La Mme poetry competition. Some of his work is published in *Poetry Potion* and *Odd Magazine*.

UBukelani Mmelly Shangase wazalwa wakhulela kwaMaphumulo KwaZulu-Natal. Ungowokuqala ezinganeni eziyisikhombisa zikaNyenyezile Shangase noMqiniseni Mali Shangase. Njengeningi labaculi walifulathela ikhaya weza eGoli ngonyaka we-1980, okunamanje usazinze khona. Usesebenze isikhathi eside endimeni yomculo womaskandi. Naba abanye babaculi balolu hlobo lomculo aseke wasebenza nabo: Umfaz' omnyaka Khumalo, Ikhansela noJBC, noFive

Roses Dlamini. Ngaphandle kokucula ukhonze ukubhala izinkondlo zesiZulu.

Siwaphiwe Fortune Shweni was born in 1995 in a small village in the Eastern Cape, Engcobo. He studied at Tshatshatsha PJS, Freemantle Boys' High School and Cape Peninsula University of Technology in the Western Cape. His work is published in *The Kalahari Review*, *Prufrock* issue 12 and on the Avbob poetry website (2017). He was one of the finalists in the 2016 McGregor poetry competition.

Francine Simon was born in 1990 in Durban to Indian Catholic parents. She recently completed her doctorate in English studies at Stellenbosch University. Her poems have been published in South African literary journals such as *New Coin* and *Aerodrome*. She launched her debut collection of poetry, *Thungachi*, in 2017. She is currently working on a new poetry project about South African Indian identity.

Tiisetso Thiba is a poet and novelist and was born in a village called Ganyesa in North West. He has written two books, a poetry book titled *Let's Take a Walk, Mama* (2015) and a Setswana novel titled *Tlhabane Ya Makgowa* (2017). Thiba has started to write more of his work in Setswana to promote and preserve his language. He has been on the SABC youth programme *Mzansi Insider* and was been featured on News24 and Beautiful News in 2017 for his Setswana book. Tiisetso is currently working as a communications officer.

Elizabeth Trew returned to South Africa in 1991 after decades out of the country. She has an MA in English education from Wits, facilitates writing workshops for

People Opposing Women Abuse (POWA) and volunteers at a shelter for girls in Cape Town. Her poems have appeared in various poetry journals in South Africa and England, a selection in *ISISx* (Botsotso) and *Prodigal Daughters: Stories of South African women in exile*, edited by Lauretta Ngcobo (UKZN Press).

Thato Tshukudu is the 2017 national winner of the Poetry in Mcgregor competition and is featured in the 2016 and 2017 *Best New African Poets Anthology*, Volume VIII of the *Sol Plaatje European Union Anthology, Better Than Starbucks, Poetry Potion*. Thato released his debut body of poetry titled *fly in a beehive* in 2018

Elna van Niekerk started her first job as a lecturer in philosophy at the University of the North, stayed on her own in the Wolkberg mountains for a few months, was a bus driver for the Tshwane City Council and then worked in Transport Safety research at the CSIR for 19 years. Currently she manages her own company. She has four children and lives in Pretoria. Recently some of her poems were accepted for publication in *Nuwe Stemme 6*.

Lester Walbrugh is from Grabouw in the Western Cape. He writes short fiction and poems and is an editorial member of Type/Cast, an online literary journal. His work has been published in the short story anthologies of the National Arts Festival and Short Story Day Africa.

Jeannie Wallace McKeown lives in Grahamstown, South Africa, and writes poetry and prose creatively. She works full-time at Rhodes University but also as a freelance writer covering academic lectures, seminars and book launches. She has had creative pieces published in literary journals and online, is the mother of two boys who can no longer be described as small and is in a steady co-parenting relationship with an ex-husband. Her collection, *Unremembered Poems*, will be published by Modjaji Books in 2018.

Crystal Warren grew up in Port Elizabeth but has lived and worked in Grahamstown for nearly 30 years. She has worked as a librarian, literary researcher and museum curator, and has always been surrounded by books. Her poems have appeared in several anthologies and journals. Her first collection, *Bodies of Glass*, appeared in 2004 and the long delayed second collection, *Predictive Text*, will come out in 2018.

Flow Wellington is the author of two self-published collections, *The Undelivered Score* and *Gau-Trained*. She is the founding owner of Poetree Publications, a company that offers African writers affordable publishing and distribution services. To date, the company has 15 titles under its belt. Flow has been published in local and international publications including *To Breathe Into Another Voice* (SA jazz anthology) and *The Atlanta Review*. She also acts as a curating consultant for the Eastern Cape Book Festival committee.

Athol Williams has published four poetry collections and his poems have been published in over 40 publications internationally. His creative and scholarly work focuses on identifying and eradicating structural barriers to social justice and celebrating humanity's great possibilities. Athol holds degrees from Oxford, Harvard, LSE, MIT, London Business School and Wits.

What is the European Union (EU)?

The European Union is a unique economic and political union between 28 European countries[1] that together cover much of the continent. The EU was created in the aftermath of the Second World War. The first steps were to foster economic cooperation: the idea being that countries that trade with one another become economically interdependent and so more likely to avoid conflict.

Since its birth, the union has developed into a huge single market with the euro as its common currency. What began as a purely economic union has evolved into an organisation spanning policy areas from climate, environment and health to external relations and security, justice and migration.

The single or 'internal' market is the EU's main economic engine, enabling most goods, services, money and people to move freely. Another key objective is to develop this huge resource also in other areas like energy, knowledge and capital markets to ensure that Europeans can draw the maximum benefit from it.

The EU is based on the rule of law: everything it does is founded on treaties, voluntarily and democratically agreed by its member countries. It actively promotes human rights and democracy and in 2012 was awarded the Nobel Peace Prize for advancing the causes of peace, reconciliation, democracy and human rights in Europe.

How does it work?
EU Member States have set up institutions to run the EU and adopt its legislation. The main ones are:
- The European Parliament (representing the people of

Europe)
- The Council of the European Union (representing national governments)
- The European Commission (representing the common EU interest)

Size & population
The EU is less than half the size of the United States covering some 4 million km². In terms of size, France is the EU's largest country and Malta its smallest. The EU has a population of close to 505 million people – the world's third largest after China and India.

The EU's economy
Operating as a single market, the EU is a major world trading power. EU economic policy seeks to sustain growth by investing in transport, energy and research while minimising the impact of further economic development on the environment. Measured in terms of the goods and services it produces, its economy is bigger than that of the US.

EU symbols
- The European flag – The 12 stars in a circle symbolise the ideals of unity, solidarity and harmony among the peoples of Europe.
- The European anthem – The melody used to symbolise the EU comes from Ludwig Van Beethoven's 9th Symphony composed in 1823.
- Europe Day – The ideas behind the EU were first put forward on 9 May 1950 by French Foreign Minister

Robert Schuman. This is why 9 May is celebrated as a key date for the EU.
- The EU motto – "United in diversity".

The EU & South Africa – a partnership of equals

Since 1994 the growing relationship between South Africa and the EU has been underpinned by the Trade, Development and Cooperation Agreement (TDCA). Closer ties between the two parties were consolidated in 2007 with the establishment of the EU-SA Strategic Partnership.

This partnership, the only one of its kind with an African country, is centred on enhanced political dialogue around issues of shared interest including climate change, the global economy, governance, bilateral trade, and peace and security matters. In line with this, its action plan encompasses sectoral cooperation on a range of issues such as climate change, environment, education, science and technology, space, trade and migration.

Regular high level meetings steer the partnership, along with the EU-South Africa Joint Cooperation Council. They provide the occasions to discuss current bilateral, regional and global issues.

Trade & investment

The EU is South Africa's most important trading partner. In 2017, according to Eurostat, the EU was the destination of some 22% (R262 bn) of total SA exports and the source of close to 30.5% (R338 bn) of total SA imports. Manufactured goods comprise a meaningful component of

SA's exports, with over half the exports to the EU leaving SA shores in processed or semi-processed form. EU countries are also the source of some 74% of foreign direct investment (FDI) stock in South Africa.

Development cooperation

The EU remains an important development partner to South Africa, providing significant external assistance funds. The EU's total indicative grant budget for South Africa for the period 2014–20 amounts to some €250 million. It is complemented by a €416 million loan finance envelope from the European Investment Bank (EIB) as well as grant funding from the EU Member States.

---

* Belgium, Bulgaria, Croatia, Czech Republic, Denmark, Germany, Estonia, Ireland, Greece, Spain, France, Italy, Cyprus, Latvia, Lithuania, Luxembourg, Hungary, Malta, the Netherlands, Austria, Poland, Portugal, Romania, Slovenia, Slovakia, Finland, Sweden, and the United Kingdom.